Advance Praise for

𝒯𝐻𝐸 𝐵𝒜𝒫 𝐻𝒜𝒩𝒟𝐵𝒪𝒪𝒦

The Official Guide to the Black American Princess

"You don't have to be a BAP to love this book. This Italian American Princess howled with laughter at this royal primer, a how-to for any girl who aspires to rule the universe."

—Adriana Trigiani, author of *Big Stone Gap*

"Every sistah has a little BAP in her, and this hilarious, on-the-money guide to these divine divas will have you howling with laughter!"

—TaRessa Stovall, coauthor of *A Love Supreme*

"Hilarious! *The BAP Handbook* has made the world safe for siddity women everywhere. Finally, we can say it loud: we're bourgie and we're proud!!!"

—Susan Fales-Hill

The BAP Handbook

THE OFFICIAL GUIDE

TO THE

BLACK AMERICAN PRINCESS

KALYN JOHNSON, TRACEY LEWIS,

KARLA LIGHTFOOT, AND

GINGER WILSON

ILLUSTRATIONS BY JANE ARCHER

Broadway Books
NEW YORK

BROADWAY

BROADWAY BOOKS and its logo, a letter B bisected on the diagonal, are trademarks of
Broadway Books, a division of Random House, Inc.

June 2001
First Edition
Designed by Diane Hobbing of Snap-Haus Graphics
Illustrated by Jane Archer
ISBN 0-7394-1816-5

To our parents, who provide us with much love

and who have generously given us carte blanche

to our regal existences.

Acknowledgments

We are thankful to have had the opportunity to chart the course for BAPs across the country. We hope our sisters—BAPs and other princesses alike—will read this book and have a chance to laugh at themselves.

All four of us are blessed with sisters with whom we share our most precious and intimate BAP experiences. Kendell; Pam, Robbyn, and Wendy; Karen; and Kelly—you all have taught us the true meaning of friendship. We love you guys unconditionally!

Many friends, old and new, were important to us while writing this book. Those of you who fielded phone calls, participated in surveys, read drafts, and helped brainstorm during dry periods (you know who you are)—we could not have done it without all of your help and support!

Thanks to Janet Hill, our editor—we're glad our book told your story! We also thank Roberta Spivak, Lisa Davis, Victoria Cook, and Lynn Hobson for their belief in our project and their patience with the four of us.

And last, we'd like to thank Oprah Winfrey, who spared a few moments on a cold and sad day in January 1997; your act of kindness propelled us on a path that culminated in the publishing of this book.

—The BAPgirls

Contents

₽REAMBLE

black amer·i·can prin·cess \'blak e-mer-e-ken 'prin(t)-ses\ *n., adj., abbr. usu. cap BAP:* a. A pampered female of African-American descent born to an upper-middle- or upper-class family. b. An African-American female whose life experiences give her a "sense of entitlement." c. An African-American female accustomed to the best and nothing less!

This book is written by Black American Princesses (BAPs), for BAPs, wanna-be BAPs, the uninitiated, and anyone mildly curious about that Black girl who is so poised and confident and seems to have everything. In fact, she really seems to be quite "JAP-py" (like that Jewish American Princess [JAP]—who is simply selective, not spoiled). *The BAP Handbook: The Official Guide to the Black American Princess* provides a satirical insight into our lives and culture in a way never before addressed.

   Any true BAP will read this book with a nod of approval. For everyone else, this book will be a guide into our social *milieu,* charting a course from birth through adulthood and beyond. Not everyone who reads this book will do so claiming to be a member, but everyone who completes the journey will be able to easily spot a BAP and even become a princess with a little hard work, extra cash, and a newfound appreciation for the finer things in life.

Princesses come in all shapes, sizes, and colors. While our book focuses on Black American Princesses, all princesses share the same intrinsic traits, which bridge the gap between our cultural differences. Our bond in the *bon vivant* revolution that we are waging at hair salons, spas, makeup counters, and major department stores around the world unites us in a lifetime of the "Best and Nothing Less."

You Might Be a BAP If . . .

- You insist on parking in illegal spaces and then wonder why your car was towed.
- You'd rather have the original or nothing at all.
- Weekend trips to Europe have become a habit.
- You know what "shopping-bag-handle cramp" is.
- You have converted one of the rooms in your house into a closet.
- It takes you an entire year to get a cleaning lady because you're still trying to clean up before she comes.
- You assume the world is your oyster.
- You date a man who lives over a thousand miles away, but you still see him every weekend (and he foots the bill).
- You have a standing weekly hair appointment.
- You're well known in all of the premium outlet stores within a one-hundred-mile radius of your home.

The BAP Test

1. What is San Pellegrino?
   a. A mountain range in Italy
   b. A bird
   c. Effervescent water
   d. A clothier

2. The House of Prada is located in
   a. Hong Kong
   b. NYC
   c. Milan
   d. Barney's

3. Mikimotos are worn
   a. Around the neck, on fingers, and in ears
   b. As kimonos
   c. On the feet
   d. As pajamas

4. The Link(s)
   a. Is slang for the golf course
   b. Are sausages
   c. Are things on a chain
   d. Is a women's service organization

5. Makeup should look
   a. Like you have it on/dramatic
   b. Natural
   c. Like warpaint
   d. Better on your face than in its container

6. **When you hear Dean & DeLuca, you think**
   a. Da-what?
   b. A bad Vegas comedy act
   c. Dolce & Gabbana's cousins
   d. A famous specialty grocery store

7. ***Peau de soie* is**
   a. French for patent leather
   b. A beautiful silk textile usually used for evening bags and shoes
   c. Spanish for leather
   d. A new perfume

8. **A BAP without a tube of MAC is like**
   a. The Louvre without *Mona Lisa*
   b. A writer without a pen
   c. Gucci without Tom Ford
   d. All of the above

9. **You are having a bad hair day and you have a date in one hour, so you**
   a. Cancel the date and reschedule it for the day of your next hair appointment
   b. Give him a pair of dark sunglasses and go to a midnight double feature
   c. Hope he doesn't notice
   d. Join the witness protection program

10. **Christmas is around the corner, so how do you get your new beau to buy your gift from Tiffany's, Barney's, or Cynthia Rowley?**
    a. You don't, he just knows where to go
    b. Tell "his boy"
    c. Subtle hints—catalogs in the bathroom
    d. Pray

11. **A man you're not interested in continues to pursue you. The thrill is gone; how do you drop him? Tell him . . .**
    a. You've joined the CIA
    b. Your husband found out about him
    c. You want to have ten kids and quit working
    d. It's been great, but you met someone else

12. **A wanna-be sees you shopping at TJ Maxx, Marshall's, or at an outlet mall. You**
    a. Lie and say your not-so-hip friend dragged you out
    b. Dodge, don't make eye contact, and pray she didn't see you
    c. Say hi, you're no dummy, why pay full price when you can get two for the price of one?
    d. Say you're looking to see if they really have the same stuff as the department stores

13. **Robert Clergerie is**
    a. A famous Black hair designer
    b. The next Richard Wright
    c. A shoe designer
    d. RuPaul's boyfriend

14. **In addition to MAC, a true BAP has at least one tube from**
    a. Stila
    b. Makeup Forever
    c. Chanel
    d. Bobbi Brown

15. **A Sunday afternoon treat is**
    a. Going to your neighborhood bookstore and getting lost among the books
    b. Meeting for lunch to gossip
    c. Having a date
    d. All of the above

16. **Dim Sum is**
    a. Ebonics for them and some
    b. Chinese brunch
    c. A perfume
    d. Einstein's theory of relativity

17. **When traveling abroad, how much luggage do you take with you?**
    a. One checked bag and a carry-on
    b. Five Louis Vuitton or Gucci suitcases
    c. You send it ahead of you
    d. Who are you calling a broad?

18. **At your college reunion you rent what type of car?**
    a. Nothing, you'll carpool with a few classmates who still live in the area
    b. A Jag, baby!
    c. Something conservative with good mileage
    d. My driver will tend to those matters

19. Kevan Hall is

   a. The Halston designer (couturier)

   b. A character from a romance novel

   c. That guy from *Saturday Night Live*

   d. Jerry Hall's distant cousin

20. Harriet Tubman is

   a. The name of the first female African American astronaut

   b. A freed slave who led many to freedom on the Underground Railroad

   c. A rapper

   d. A new shoe designer

15+ points Congrats! You are officially a BAP, now go get your MAC tube of lipstick. 10–15 points A BAP maybe, or darn close. 5–10 points Read this book very very carefully and we guarantee that your score will improve. 0–5 points Pick up a copy of *You Know You're Ghetto When . . .*

THE BABY BAP ANTHEM

HEY THERE, HEY THERE, LITTLE BAP

(Sung to the tune of "Twinkle, Twinkle, Little Star")

Hey there, hey there, little BAP
Can't mistake you for a JAP
A star in your parents' eyes
You can have the moon and sky

Hey there, hey there, little BAP
With your perfect shoes and cap.

THE BIRTH OF A BAP

The lights are bright, the camera is rolling, and both the baby BAP and her mother are screaming. Her parents, with the help of an expert team of doctors, escort her to center stage. It is her greatest entrance of all. This is why to this day she feels that those around her should celebrate her birthday as if it were a national holiday. Still protesting her untimely eviction from the womb—the ultimate condo—the baby BAP begins her quest to solve the major mysteries of her new life. With the abrupt end to her food supply and a totally unnecessary smack on the tush from a green-masked stranger, questions pop into her inquiring mind: What's going on? Where am I? How will I eat? Who will pay for my Ivy League education? Who will buy my clothes? I want Prada. I want Kate Spade. Jewelry? Cars? And my wedding? I want a Vera Wang wedding dress.

Amidst the commotion there is a moment of calm as father and daughter see one another for the first time. She gurgles and smiles as she is handed over to him; unbeknownst to both of them, she has just succeeded in wrapping him around her tiny little finger for life. At that very moment, her father vows that his little princess will have a regal existence and never want for anything.

Little does her father know that his pledge will cost him hundreds of thousands of dollars. Little does she know that her magical spell over him will result in a lifetime of zealous overprotection. Without enunciating a syllable, this demanding waif telepathically transmits her desires to her parents. Now, they will do anything to give her the "perfect" life—trips abroad, membership in the most coveted organizations, nice cars and homes, a closetful of beautiful clothes, and a top-notch education.

A creature like no other, she demands the Best and Nothing Less. She is the BAP, the Black American Princess!

BAPitude

BAPitude, the BAP mind-set, starts before she can even talk and only escalates after that. Her arrival home from the hospital marks the beginning of a life full of the Best and Nothing Less. Eager to provide their daughter with endless possibilities, her parents' first task is to ensure that she is fully equipped to meet life's challenges. So, the BAP's first housewarming gift is a solid value system.

The BAP is raised to be a respectful and considerate person. She may have a selfish moment or two (okay, or three or four) but she quickly learns that her parents will not tolerate it. Spoiled? Yes. Overindulged? Yes. Obnoxious and intolerable? No, never! Her BAParents, like the TV Huxtables, don't play that. Many-a-time she will be told, "That may be how those little girls you go to school with act, but that's not acceptable behavior in this household!" By hook or by crook, her parents instill their little girl with qualities that teach her to be a princess regardless of her material possessions and worldly experiences.

Surprisingly, this overindulged young child who has been tempered by pragmatism and love blossoms into a well-balanced individual. She is taught that BAPitude does not give her license to run roughshod over others. Imbued with a sense of largesse, the BAP remains grounded and appreciative of her charmed existence.

Etiquette, Schmediquette

Etiquette, schmediquette, some might say. But etiquette is a sign of proper breeding, as any true BAP knows. BAPs don't broadcast who they are, what they have, or how they got it . . . such behavior goes against their earliest etiquette lessons from *maman*. As she grows up, the BAP discovers that her knowledge of etiquette rivals that of Miss Manners.

A BAP without good home training is like red beans without rice. The recipe for home training calls for a pinch of domestic arts (with a little help from the housekeeper), along with a cup of civic duty, three table-spoons of common sense, and a quart of maternal admonitions. The foremost ingredient in this recipe is to uphold the family name. To do otherwise is tantamount to committing treason on the most sacred of institutions, the BAP family. On the rare occasion when the BAP "shows out" at home . . . she *might* be able to get away with it. But one false move in public and you know the rest! The BAP's goal is to leave only good thoughts in the minds of those whose paths she crosses.

I Say Potato, You Say Po-Tah-Toe. . . .

Despite her parents' best intentions to give their child a worry-free life, the BAP is placed in the precarious position of living in two differ-ent worlds: one full of mashed potatoes, the other full of sweet pota-toes. In her mashed potato world, whites are repeatedly awed and impressed by how "articulate" she is and usually fail to realize that, like them, she'd be at a loss in the heart of the projects. And unfortu-nately, in her sweet potato world, Blacks often view her as pretentious and elitist. No matter the choice of spud, the BAP always reigns tri-umphant. She refuses to allow the new potatoes of the world (or the old potatoes for that matter) to keep her eyes off the prize. Their mis-conceptions about the BAP only serve to intensify her focus.

The great unwashed masses' perception of the BAP is as twisted as Bob Jones University's dating policy. Simply because the BAP leads a privileged life, she is believed to be shallow and materialistic. In fact, you probably think that the only meaningful contribution a BAP can make to society is a perfectly color-coordinated, designer-label closet! Sure, a BAP loves the finer things in life—who doesn't? But the BAP is more than a "material girl," she finds time in her busy schedule to give back to her community.

The greatest misconception about BAPs is that these dynamic individuals are all alike. This belief is heresy in the High Holy Church of All Things Expensive! But for the unconverted, the sacred truth is that there are actually four different kinds of BAPs: two by birthright—the Betty and the Boho, one by ascension—the Butterfly, and one by misappropriation—the Bogus. As you read, please keep in mind that most BAPs do not fit neatly into one category.

BAP Oath

Membership is priceless. Before one becomes a platinum card-carrying BAP, she must memorize this oath and take it to heart:

I, _____, do solemnly swear to uphold the morals and ideals of my forebears; to have my hair done on a regular basis (special dispensation for Boho); to blaze new trails for BAPs everywhere, and to lift (those around me) as I climb (as long as no one steps on my Clergeries).

I also promise to abide by the Nine Nevers. I will:

NEVER embarrass my family,

NEVER flaunt my wealth and privileges,

NEVER wear holey underwear,

NEVER accept less than one carat,

NEVER wear nail decals,

NEVER have gold teeth,

NEVER date a man with a press and curl,

NEVER let them see me sweat,

And I Will Never Expect Anything Less than the Best!

Now stand up, raise your MAC lipstick tube to the sky, and repeat the following:

Say it loud, I'm a BAP and I'm proud!
Say it loud, I'm a BAP and I'm proud!
Say it loud, I'm a BAP and I'm proud!

A BUPPY Is Not a BAP

Another general misconception is that every Black educated professional woman is a BAP. The terms BAP and Black Urban Professional (BUPPY) are not interchangeable. A BAP may also be "categorized" as BUPPY, but a BUPPY is not necessarily a BAP. BAPitude is about one's lifestyle, a way of thinking. Some argue that one's professional status catapults one into the BAP lifestyle, but such advocates are misguided. Being a BAP is about more than one's job or the size of one's bank account. There is not enough money in the world to purchase BAPitude.

Top Ten Maternal Admonitions

1. Oh no! You aren't going out of the house looking like that!
2. Don't embarrass me.
3. Don't act out.
4. Is that how you're going to wear your hair?
5. Now what do you say? (Thank you.)
6. I'm talking! What do you say? (Excuse me.)
7. (When visiting a friend.) You better show them you were raised properly and clean up after yourself. I didn't raise any heathens.
8. Cross your legs at the ankles.
9. You'll be grown soon enough. Go upstairs and wash that eyeliner off before someone sees you.
10. Stand up straight. Hold your stomach in. Tuck your butt under.

Betty

Betty: Mirror, Mirror, on the wall, who's the BAPpiest of them all?

Mirror: Why *you* are, my dear, with your perfect life, let's just hope you don't crack before you become a wife!

bet·ty \'bede, 'bete, -i\ *n., usu. cap B [short for continuous betterment]:* a. A BAP by birthright who strives for perfection in everything she undertakes. b. A BAP whose life expectations are based on a sense of entitlement. c. The quintessential BAP.

Perfection to her is quite essential
She has to live up to her potential.
She works real hard, all day and
night,
To get it
And do it,
'Cuz the Betty wants it right!

No pretender to the throne, Betty is the BAPpiest of all. Firm in the belief that her lifestyle is a right guaranteed by birth, her demeanor is infused with a regal air. As a child of privilege, Betty has always received and expected the Best and Nothing Less. Her birthright guarantees unlimited access to the world.

Betty's vanity, her compulsive shopping, and workout schedule give some the impression that she is a narcissistic shop-a-holic, but nothing could be further from the truth. Well, there might be a modicum of truth here. . . . A few Bettys have made curler confessions. Yes, they admitted to putting curlers in their hair once their boyfriends had fallen asleep. And believe it or not, they woke up extra-early to take them out (if they admitted to this, imagine what they won't 'fess up to!).

Nevertheless, despite this teeny-tiny flaw, Bettys are overachievers who recognize that they are fortunate to live the lives they do. Non-BAPs see Betty's existence as one of excess, but Betty is not embarrassed by her lifestyle or how others may perceive it; this attitude is often mistaken for arrogance or snobbery. Put simply, her parents raised her to believe that the world is her oyster, and Betty simply cannot imagine living any other way.

Betty lives by the Four P's: Precision, Perfection, Patience, and Persistence. She constantly strives for precision and perfection using patience and persistence in everything that she does, and she always comes out on top. She expects the Best and Nothing Less from everyone she encounters: skycaps, waitresses, salespeople, and of course her family and friends. Betty may not see immediate results, and she may even face a few setbacks, but she knows it's just a matter of adhering to the Four P's. Whether it is the "perfect" job, "perfect" house, "perfect" vacation, or "perfect" man, Betty is on a constant quest for, what else? Perfection.

Neurotic? Anal? Compulsive? All three are fair descriptions, but these qualities also endear Betty to those who know and love her. She is used to getting what she wants, when she wants, and how she wants it. This demanding attitude is the result of her overindulgent childhood. What else is a little girl supposed to think when her mother refuses to buy her another pair of funky jeans, but her shop-a-phobic father brings them home a day later? Naturally, she believes "I want" equals "I get."

Betty is burdened with numerous expectations, namely: securing a suitable career and an acceptable life mate. The quest for these Holy Grails begins at a young age with a strong emphasis on academics and proper socialization. Her mother helps her design the obstacle course to her heart. Meanwhile, her father, as overprotective as ever, suggests that she choose a career that will make her self-sufficient. (For the Betty who does not heed this advice, please see the Boho section.)

Climbing the ladder of success does not daunt Betty in the slightest, to her there is no such thing as a glass ceiling. With that worldview, it's no wonder Bettys are found in high-powered positions in business, law, politics, and medicine. Naturally, she gravitates toward these positions—how else could she live in the style to which she's become accustomed?

Betty's lifestyle requires that she look the part of whatever role she's thrust into, from the boardroom to the bedroom. The key word in fashion for Bettys is "understated." Whether a Betty is a classic, funky, or chic dresser, she always wears the right thing. With her wide circle of friends and endless events to attend, she must look good at all times.

Despite her cool, calm, and always well-dressed demeanor, Betty can be one stressed-out sister in her constant quest for perfection. However, Bettys learn to deal with this stress quite well—so well, in fact, that no one has any idea of the amount they deal with on a daily basis. Betty has received subtle and not-so-subtle hints from her parents that others should think that her life is "perfect." Attempting to please her parents and appear "perfect" can be taxing on even the

Bettiest of Bettys, but she suffers in silence. Don't get her wrong! Betty has an unfailing wellspring of inner resourcefulness, and, trust us, she does know how to blow off some steam and party!

Betty is usually so busy "bettering" herself that she rarely takes the time to listen to her inner voice telling her to slow down . . . think . . . do what *she* wants. Finding a balance between doing the "right" thing and enjoying herself is something Betty learns to master as she matures. Growing up, going to college, her first job, or, for some, marriage gives Betty the opportunity to shine on her own without the aid of her loving parents. As their influence wanes, she begins to trust her inner voice. Perfection, while still important, takes a backseat to happiness.

Vanity is her vice, Tiffany & Co. is her friend. Perfection, punctuated with hard work and determination, afford her this end!

Boho

Boho: Mirror, Mirror, on the wall, who is the most free-spirited BAP of all?

Mirror: *You* are, dear, with your lifestyle choice, you *always* listen to your inner voice!

bo·ho \'bo-ho\ *n., usu. cap B [diminutive of bohemian]:* a. A BAP by birthright who lives an unorthodox lifestyle. b. A funky-fresh sister with a decidedly unique if not outrageous approach to life. c. A majorette in her one-woman band.

Boho marches to the funky beat of a different drummer. Upon first glance, one may be tempted to call Boho "granola" or "artsy-fartsy." And she is. But that's only half the story. Her mellow demeanor, eclectic tastes in clothing and hair, and bohemian lifestyle are just as much a testament to her BAPpiness as her parents' bank account! So, despite the exterior, what's the difference between Boho and Betty? Although Boho enjoys all the rights and benefits that accrue to platinum card-carrying BAPs, she remains untethered by the earthly demands of her sister, Betty.

But how can Boho claim BAPhood when she refuses to toe the party line? It's easy. She's a free spirit whose notion of perfection comes from within. Boho is determined to find what truly makes her happy, and not what her family or friends expect. This often compels her to defy authority. "A rule?" she asks, "What's that?" Following directions has been problematic for her from day one.

In the Boho war for independence, childhood is the first battleground where parent and child face off. It starts with a small skirmish. Say the baby Boho refuses to wear a new Oilily dress without a pair of shorts underneath. She and her mother will duke it out before her mother concedes (one for Boho, zero for the BAParent). From there, the battles escalate to where she wants to go to camp or college. When it comes down to it, the battles center around Boho's freedom of expression. Her prowess on the battlefield shows Boho that the world does not come to a screeching halt when she fails to follow her parents' rules. So, breaking one rule leads to breaking another and another and another. And, before you know it, Boho is the victor!

Hair is another avenue of self-expression for the Boho. While thoroughly trained in the ways of BAP hair as a child, as a young adult Boho openly rebels against the Hare Krishna-like hair indoctrination of her youth. She now renounces the insidious invasion of chemicals in her hair. Instead, she prefers to let it reign in all its natural glory whether it be "free" or in braids, twists, or locks. These hairstyles are problematic for BAP mothers, who feel their daughters are rejecting their mantra: "Your hair is your crown and glory." Boho merely feels that her crown should express her roots!

Being a Boho is not as simple as she makes it appear. She's capable of weathering high-pressured situations or graduate school, but finds her muse sagging under the weight of societal and familial expectations. See, Boho doesn't thrive on stress . . . it's not her thing.

Everyone deals with stress in her own way; Boho just chooses not to deal with it if she can help it. So rather than suffer the slings and arrows of outrageous fortune, her inner percussionist leads her to a world filled with peace, love, and soooooooul!!!

This present-day flower child can be found working in any area that has a relaxed dress code and a less corporate atmosphere. Often you will find Bohos as writers, teachers, producers, artists, social workers, public defenders, or in any job that bucks the system or has a cause behind it. This calling to serve the public assuages her guilt for inheriting the first pew at the High Holy Church of All Things Expensive. Although Boho expects to live a comfortable lifestyle, she isn't focused on making a ton of money—just enough to purchase as many Birkenstocks as her little heart desires!

Just because she wears Birkies doesn't mean she renounces her BAP membership. She simply wouldn't be caught dead without the requisite Boho trappings or her BAPitude. When it comes to clothing, Bohos either shine or fail miserably. While no particular theme resonates throughout her wardrobe, one note is loud and clear . . . it must appear as if she did not spend an inordinate amount of time or money on her outfit. While the exact opposite is usually the case, a casual observer would be none the wiser. Mothers, of course, pray that their Boho's eccentric taste in clothing is a phase that will eventually pass.

So, traversing through life composing her song, Boho must remain steadfast and carve out her own niche. Let Boho march to the sound she hears, however measured or far away, just as long as she keeps the beat.

Butterfly

Butterfly: Mirror, Mirror, on the wall, who is the most grounded BAP of all?

Mirror: Why *you* are, dear, with your realistic life—you've persevered and excelled in spite of strife!

But·ter·fly: \'be·ter·fli\ *n., usu. cap B:* a. A BAP who evolved from a dormant state at any point during her life. b. A BAP who is often presumed to be a Betty. c. A BAP who may protest the categorization.

If Cinderella were Black, she'd be a Butterfly. The Butterfly knows what life is like after the clock strikes midnight—no ride, no man, no fly glass slippers. While she isn't born dripping with diamonds, she is born with a huge dose of steely perseverance. Through sheer will, accented with a little good fortune, she turns into a lovely BAP. Her two delightful sisters Betty and Boho are there to guide her each step of the way. While college usually provides the catalyst for the Butterfly's metamorphosis, the crux of her story begins at birth.

See, Butterfly is born to be a Betty, but she didn't grow up with the same fairy-tale beginning. Don't be mistaken. Just because she's a late bloomer doesn't mean she is a second-class BAP. *Au contraire!* In fact, Butterfly has an advantage over starry-eyed Bettys and Bohos; her humble beginnings nourish a grounded, mature BAP. Raised in a home with chitterlings, spice, and everything nice, Butterfly is often confronted with life's realities. She knows the value of a dollar and *works* for her allowance, unlike Betty and Boho, who, with the help of the housekeeper, merely go through the motions to collect their weekly stipends.

Butterfly's parents also want the best for their little girl, it's just that providing it sometimes proves to be difficult. Nevertheless, Butterfly is reared with the belief that a college education is the "equalizing elixir," the stepping-stone from obscurity to influence and power. Going to college grants her the opportunity to become whatever she wants: a doctor, lawyer, professor, accountant, the list is endless. Her achievements are limited only by her dreams. She goes to college and acquires the BAP knowledge.

Butterfly's metamorphosis usually begins in college (but it can start as early as junior high school or for the fortunate Butterfly in elementary school). Butterfly attends the "right" schools, hangs out with the "right" crowd, joins the "right" sororities, and dates the "right" men. The Butterfly's exposure to many of these experiences is by happenstance. Perhaps it is the friendship she strikes up with her college roommate, the interest she has in art history, or the young man who takes her to the theater. She watches how those around her dress, wear their hair, and carry themselves. An inquisitive soul, Butterfly is not afraid to ask for advice when she truly needs it. Her questions may range from "What should I wear to the Black and Gold Ball?" to "What's the difference between brie and camembert?" Her motto in life is "There's no such thing as a dumb question," and she's right. Her experiences and friendships increase Butterfly's base of knowledge about herself and the world.

While Butterfly's training on the ins and outs of BAPdom is top-notch, she regresses from time to time. To keep her in the proper BAP mind-set, Betty and Boho jokingly chastise her occasional misstep, but in the end, however, she passes her finishing lessons with flying colors.

Nevertheless, Butterfly will protest until collards are no longer green that she is not a BAP, but she is. Her outcry signifies that Butterfly never forgets where she came from, acts pretentious, or tries to pretend that she, or her family, is something she is not. Butterfly makes no apologies for her modest background and resents those who do. This honesty and integrity distinguish Butterfly from Bogus.

Beyond the age of twenty-one, it can be difficult to distinguish Butterflies from Bettys. Four years of college acclimates and comfortably ensconces Butterflies in the BAP lifestyle; they've got more BAPitude than some Bettys and Bohos (but hey, they learned from the best). Just as the fairy godmother's magic wand transforms Cinderella, college graduation allows Butterfly to emerge from her cocoon, spread her wings, and take flight.

Bogus

Bogus: Mirror, Mirror, on the wall, who's the most genuine BAP of all?

Mirror: *Not you,* not you, not you, my dear. You're too busy hiding behind your expensive gear.

bo•gus \'bo-ges\ *n., usu. cap B:* a. An imposter who is not an authentic BAP. b. Her BAP status is a figment of her imagination. c. A greedy gut.

(Based on the nursery rhyme "Mary, Mary, Quite Contrary")
Bogus, Bogus, quite misleading
How do you get through life?
With overextended credit, you just don't get it
We sure hope Bogus isn't your wife!

The story of Bogus BAP is a pathetic one! Hers is a tale of woe. Bogus gives BAPs a bad name because she personifies the stereotypes that haunt BAPs. (You know, all of the things you thought about BAPs before you started reading this book.) Bogus, as her name connotes, doesn't understand the first thing about being a BAP. She defines herself by her appearance and her material possessions. She just doesn't have a clue!

When Bogus is born, her parents, like most, want to give her the world. She too is treated like a princess, but her parents' misguided priorities send Bogus the wrong message. She may grow up with a closet full of nice clothes and the latest video games, but check out the family homestead. Instead of repairing the toilet that runs incessantly or the plaster that's falling off the walls, they spend their money on "things" for their daughter. They want her to be like other BAPs and believe that if she has certain items, her social status will rise. As a result, keeping up with the Joneses and social climbing, at any cost, are Bogus's only extracurricular activities. Too bad the Joneses don't care (and neither do the Johnsons, the Smiths, the Browns, the Lewises, or the Woods. . .).

What's important to Bogus other than her appearance and material possessions? Why, proclaiming who she knows, what she has, when she got it, where she got it, and why she thinks it's important. The fact that you have no interest in her or her stories never registers. She's just busy chatting away, hoping to leave a lasting impression. She generally does, albeit a negative one. Her talk is cheap!

While she may look, act, dress, and have the same job as a Betty, watch out, she's really a counterfeit. This poor, misguided soul is truly a wolf in sheep's clothing. The next time you go out, just look for the most ostentatious person there. She's probably wearing insignia-drenched designer clothing and is busy looking everyone up and down. Have no fear you've found her . . . she's just like the best imitation Chanel bag you've ever seen!

Today, Bogus leaves her dining room table set with fine china and crystal for all to see—but take a look in her garage. Why is her garage door always shut? Why does she always catch a ride with someone else? Is her car truly in the shop? Or is that new Jeep she just bought a figment of her imagination? Or does she really have a "jacked-up hoopty" that she only drives late at night?

A Few Famous BAPs

Betty, Boho, Butterfly, and, yes, even Bogus BAPs are prevalent among famous individuals. Whether they know it or not, the following women are BAPs. We will leave it up to you to classify them properly.

Amsale	Wedding designer
Tyra Banks	Model/actress
Halle Berry	Actress
Bertice Berry	Author/sociologist/comedian/ inspirational speaker
Beonyce	Singer/actress
Yvette Lee Bowser	TV producer
Brandi	Actress/singer
Toni Braxton	Singer
Connie Briscoe	Author
Marie Brown	Literary agent
A'lelia Bundles	TV news producer; Madame C. J. Walker's great-granddaughter
Naomi Campbell	Model
Diahann Carroll	Actress
Veronica Chambers	Author
Debra Martin Chase	Film producer
Faith Hampton Childs	Literary agent
Rev. Dr. Arlene Churn	Baptist minister/therapist
Caroline V. Clarke	Journalist/author
Corynne Corbett	Magazine editor in chief
Suzanne de Passe	Producer
Carmen deLavallade	Dancer

Norma Jean and Carol Darden	Authors/restaurateurs
Stacy Dash	Actress
Angela Davis	Activist/author
Katherine Dunham	Dancer/choreographer
Tracey Edmonds	Film producer
Tamla Edwards	Journalist
Jocelyn Elders	Former U.S. Surgeon General
Susan Fales-Hill	TV writer/producer
Ann Fudge	Businesswoman
Althea Gibson	First African American to win Wimbledon
Thelma Golden	Deputy museum director
Monique Greenwood	Magazine editor in chief
Jasmine Guy	Singer/actress
Bethann Hardison	Agent
Anita Hill	Attorney/professor
Lauryn Hill	Singer/actress
Heather Vincent Holley	TV News VP
Diane Hudson	TV producer
Cathy Hughes	Businesswoman
Gwen Ifil	TV news anchor/political talk show host
Iman	Model/entrepreneur
Yolanda Joe	Author
Beverly Johnson	Model
Marion Jones	Track and field star/Olympic gold medalist
Star Jones	Talk show host/attorney
Loretha Jones	TV producer
Tracey Kemble	TV producer
Jackie Joyner Kersee	Track and field star; Olympian
Chaka Khan	Singer

Regina King	Actress
Eartha Kitt	Actress/singer
Gladys Knight	Singer
Patti LaBelle	Singer/actress
Sanaa Lathan	Actress
Tonya Lee	TV/film producer
Kacy Lemmons	Film director
Ananda Lewis	V.J.
Abbey Lincoln	Singer
Nia Long	Actress
Marilyn McCoo	Singer
Tanya McKinnon	Literary agent
S. Epatha Merkerson	Actress
Jill Nelson	Journalist/author
Jessye Norman	Opera singer
Stephanie Stokes Oliver	Author/on-line magazine editor-in-chief
Karen Parsons	Actress
Saundra Parks	Businesswoman
Queen Latifah	Actress/musician/producer/talk show host
Sylvia Rhone	Record company chairman
Condoleeza Rice	National Security Advisor to the President
Holly Robinson-Peet	Actress
Malaak Rock	Non-profit volunteer
Tracey Ross	Actress
Salt and Pepa	Singers
Carole Simpson	TV news reporter/anchor
Lowery Stokes Sims	Museum director
Ruth Simmons	University president
B. Smith	Model/restaurateur/author

Jada Pinkett Smith	Actress
Susan Taylor	Editorial director
Veronica Webb	Model/actress
Serena Williams	Tennis player
Terrie Williams	Publicist/author
Venus Williams	Tennis player/Wimbledon winner
Oprah Winfrey	Talk show host/producer/entrepreneur
Sylvia Woods	Restaurateur
Deborah Wright	Bank president

BAP Legends

Marian Anderson	Singer (First Black to sing with the Metropolitan Opera)
Pearl Bailey	Singer/actress
Josephine Baker	Singer/civil rights activist/actress
Mary McLeod Bethune	Educator
Bessie Coleman	Pilot
Dorothy Dandridge	Actress
Ella Fitzgerald	Singer
Billie Holiday	Singer
Zora Neale Hurston	Writer/folklorist/anthropologist
Wilma Rudolph	Track and field Olympian
Sojourner Truth	Abolitionist/activist
Harriet Tubman	Abolitionist/Underground Railroad conductor
Madame C. J. Walker	Entrepreneur
Dorothy West	Writer
Phillis Wheatley	Poet

BAP Quiz #1

At an after-five charity function, while waiting for the program to commence, a woman at the BAP's table turns to the BAP and says, "I love your dress!" Please match the response to the proper BAP:

1. This? I got it out of my sister's closet.
2. Really? Thanks. I was at Saks the other day and picked it up while whisking through the Moschino section. I thought it'd be perfect for this event. I just wish it had been on sale.
3. Thanks, I like it too! It's such a fun dress!
4. Really, I wasn't sure I liked it at first. If it weren't for my friend Robyn, I probably wouldn't have bought it.

Answer Key:
1. Boho   2. Bogus   3. Betty   4. Butterfly

THE BAP IN TRAINING
Life Is Not a Dress Rehearsal

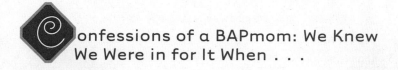

onfessions of a BAPmom: We Knew
We Were in for It When . . .

". . . she would only eat off of

her Wedgwood baby dishes with

her silver spoon from Tiffany's."

". . . at the age of four,

my eldest, Emory, exclaimed,

'Mommy, I can get Daddy to do what-

ever I want.' "

". . . little Paige had her own personal shopper at Bloomingdale's by age ten."

". . . asked at her first-grade parent-teacher conference, 'What is Courtney's reaction when she doesn't get something she wants?' And, my husband responded, 'Courtney *always* gets what she wants.' "

Shakespeare was partially correct when he said, "Life is but a stage and we are merely players." But ol' Will never met a BAP! She's no understudy and her life is no dress rehearsal. Don't slam her "Tony" award-winning performance, it's all the director's fault—the BAParent.

While BAParents know exactly what they are getting themselves into when they decide to procreate, unwittingly they raise the standard for the upbringing of young Black women across the country. As they take their seats in the directors' chair, scripts in hand, BAParents set forth to guarantee that their daughter will snag the ultimate award . . . a starring role in a life full of love, leisure, and the like.

BAParents know that the future of their princess is determined by their unflappable dispositions, names, neighborhoods, educations, and fashionable wardrobes. BAPs are meant to change the world. So what if the revolution happens on the floors of Saks Fifth Avenue. Change is change!!!

BAPNames

Choosing the right name for their little princess is the first and most important task for any BAParent. (BAP Note: While "Princess" is a cute nickname, it is a totally inappropriate BAPname.) Names suggested by persistent friends and family members are popular choices, but BAParents will never, ever choose a name that links their child to fruit, a cartoon character, a car (Portia is a Shakespearean character, not a turbocharged 911), or the backwoods of Alabama (aka Bama). From whichever source, the Baby BAP's name will have character.

Acceptable BAPNames

Akieva, Alexa, Alexis, Alicia, Allison, Amy, Andrea, Angela, Angelique, Anita, Ann, April, Ashley, Austin, Beth, Billie, Blythe, Brittany, Brooke, Caitlin, Cameron, Camille, Candice, Carla, Carmen, Carson, Cecily,

Charise, Chelsea, Chloe, Christina, Claudette, Claudia, Corinne, Courtney, Dana, Daniella, Dawn, Deborah, Denise, Devon, Elizabeth, Ellen, Emory, Ensa, Erika, Erin, Eve, Evin, Faithe, Gabriella, Gabrielle, Gayle, Gina, Ginger, Gwen, Heather, Hillary, Imani, India, Ingrid, Jacqueline, Janet, Jasmine, Jean, Jeneane, Jenna, Jennifer, Jill, Jillian, Joelle, Joy, Julia, Julie, Kalyn, Karen, Karla, Kathy, Katlin, Kaye, Kayla, Kelly, Kendall, Kendell, Kennedy, Kimberly, Kirra, Kirsten, Kitty, Kristen, Kyla, Kyra, Laura, Laurel, Lauryn, Leslie, Linda, Lindsey, Lisa, Liza, Lydia, Lynn, Madison, Maria, Marlene, Martha, Maya, McKenzie, Meagan, Meg, Megan, Melanie, Melissa, Michelle, Mimi, Monique, Morgan, Murphy, Nia, Nicole, Nikki, Octavia, Olivia, Paige, Pamela, Patrice, Patricia, Peggy, Portia, Rachel, Rebecca, Roberta, Robin, Rose Ann, Sarah, Shannon, Sharon, Shelby, Shelly, Simone, Stacey, Stephanie, Susan, Sydney, Sylvia, Tanya, Theresa, Toni, Tracey, Valerie, Vanessa, Vera, Veronica, Wendelyn, Wendy, Whitney, Yolanda, Yolande, Yvonne, and Zoe.

Taking It to the Street—Non-BAPNames

You've heard them and snickered. You've seen them spelled out and wondered what poor misguided woman thought to name her daughter LaTrine. Some folks don't know better, others are trying to be creative. Whatever the source, the end result is a mess! Any name beginning with "La" or "Sh" and ending in -ima, -ika, -isha, and -ita is never considered by BAParents. (BAP Note: If you are a Butterfly and find your name on this list, consider having it legally changed.)

Absolutely Inappropriate BAPNames

Abc (pronounced Abeecie), Akhia, Alize, Allante, Alove, Aquanetta, Arboreeta, Atavias, Camray, Caprice, Caribou, Carleisha, Chanse (pronounced Chance), Charquis, Chevodkalee, Chiquita, Cliffondra, Clintinisha, Courteney, Cressida, Curtisha, Delandra, Denisha, Deshunna, Donecka, Donika, Donniece, Duarelia, Elease, Female (pronounced

Femalay), Heavenlee, Ikoneisha, Jamita, Jaquita, Jazzmaine, Joe-juniia (pronounced joe-juana), Kanika, Kelithia, Kenietha, Kentavia, Kevinaletta, Kokeitha, LaJamicka, Lakita, Laquana, Laquisha, Laquita, LaShanda, Latia, LaTrine, Lemonjello (Orangejello's sister), Letrice, Letricia, Lexus, Lovea, Mahogany, Malibu (Caribou's twin), Markuita, Marshawn, Miprecious, Mizpha, Moleca, Nastassja, Nikita, Nyeshia, Obsession, Octavius, Orangejello, Paprika, Paradise, Peaches, Precious, Princess, Qiana, Quenjana, Ratreena, Rhondria, Riunite, Sapphire, Seneequa, Seqwana, Shakela, Shameesha, Shameka, Shaniqua, Shaquita, Shateena, Shemiah, Shenette, Sherika, Specia'l, Tanquery, Tanzela, Tawana, Tawanda, Tequila, Tinisha, Tonetta, Tonika, Tonisha, Tykenzi, Vagina (pronounced Virginia), Vaneesha.[1]

Cafe Chocolate

Life is like a latte, and most poor souls are drinking Sanka! A coffee bean can become fine espresso or freeze-dried—the difference is how it's cultivated. The growth of a BAP is similar to the creation of a fine blend of funky coffee, and BAParents ensure that the mixture is just right. Why risk sending their daughter to the freeze-dried section? They must take the time to blend and brew a good Baby BAP if they want her to be more than an average cup of joe. BAParents are more than baristas for the exclusive BAP blend, they are also her:

1. Cultural Curators
2. Athletic Directors
3. Fashion Coordinators
4. Educational Consultants
5. Social Directors

[1]Unfortunately, all these names are real.

Exposure to positive cultural elements like classical and jazz concerts (never forget your roots!), museums, and fine dining create a fertile ground from which Baby BAP blossoms. Her wardrobe encompasses outfits for all occasions: rites of passage ceremonies, bar mitzvahs, sweet sixteens, country club parties, nights out to the theater, and slumber parties. Due to meticulous parental planning, Baby BAP's curriculum vitae is the envy of everyone! Socializing with the "right" crowd reveals a sacred truth: it's not what you know, but who you know. A BAParent's job is never done!

A BAP's Letter to Santa

Dear Santa Claus,

I've been a very good girl this year. I am doing very well in school. So far I have all A's. I try not to fight with Brooke (only a little bit when she picks on me). I clean up my room for the housekeeper. Mommy gets mad when I leave my clothes on the floor. I still don't understand why I have to clean up for the housekeeper. I hope you think I was a good girl too. On the next five pages you'll find my complete Christmas list. I hope you can bring me everything . . . especially since I've been such a good girl.

Love,
The Best Little BAP in the World
Betty

ABC—As Easy as Un, Deux, Trois

War is an overpriced tea party in comparison to educating a BAP. This battle (whose final objective is an Ivy League education) requires the strategic ability of Colin Powell, the social connections of the Kennedys, the wallet of a Rockefeller, and the patience of Job.

While other parents labor under the mistaken belief that where their daughters attend kindergarten has no bearing on her college choices, BAParents know better. They move into the right neighborhoods that are brimming over with parks, good neighbors, and schools. If a bastion of BAPitude is not within Daimler distance, then magnet, parochial, or Montessori schools can provide the underpinnings for her future success.

Baby BAP sails through her primary school years with flying colors—mainly due to her top-notch home training. By the time she enters kindergarten, she can read Dr. Seuss, count to one hundred, monopolize a conversation, and even *parler un petit peu de français.* Born in the age of standardized tests, these skills guarantee her admittance to the nation's finest nursery schools. From there she graduates to the first grade, where her coloring, finger painting, and imaginative storytelling skills are further honed to prepare her for life's challenges. Baby BAP is well on the way to the top of her class!

Dear Diary,

I can't believe I'm about to start the 6th grade! But I know I'm ready. I read the best book this summer while I was at Grandma Effie's down in Arkansas, it's called I Know Why the Caged Bird Sings. This lady who's on Oprah a lot wrote it. I told my cousin Jenna that I'm going to be famous like Oprah or Maya Angelou I'm not sure what I'm going to be yet but Mommy says I can be whatever I want, if I put my mind to it.

OK, I gotta go because I want to jump double dutch before the street-lights go on. Only 8 more days 'til school starts.

Love,
Bonita Butterfly

P.S. I think when I'm grown I'm gonna change my name to Blythe—isn't it cool? I asked Mom and Dad to start calling me Blythe and they said no and that I need to be proud of who I am and live up to the name they gave me. I guess they're right but I still like Blythe better than Bonita.

She's Got *The Look*

You know it. You've seen it. Every Black mother has it. It's a look that will bring tears to the Baby BAP's eyes in seconds. No sounds, no words . . . just *The Look.* Thanks to *The Look,* few BAParents have to resort to spanking their princess's royal behind. Passed down for gen-erations, when a BAP mother disapproves of her Baby BAP's actions, she resorts to *The Look.* First, the upper lip tightens. Then she raises an eyebrow, she may even tilt her head ever so slightly and Presto, there it is: *The Look.* She'll give it anywhere, from any distance—in church, the grocery store, or at home. Wherever and whenever *The Look* is given you can be sure the Baby BAP's knees will buckle, her heart will skip a beat, and she will snap into shape faster than the speed of light.

Levels of *The Look*

1. Okay, you're cute, but calm down.
2. You're working my last nerve.
3. All right now, I'm about to paddle your behind!

Busy Bee, Busy BAP

Lessons for Her Highness

Always buzzing about, Baby BAP's day doesn't come to a screeching halt when the final bell rings. After-school activities allow her to explore her athletic, artistic, or academic interests. These endeavors keep her impressionable mind focused on its only subliminal goal—no, not boys—of getting into a prestigious high school and then a top-notch college. The BAP's AV (activity vitae) proudly exhibits her kaleidoscopic self and reveals the contribution she'd make to *any* school.

Music

No BAP can escape music lessons. Baby BAP's practice sessions can cause ear damage, stress, and heart palpitations in unsuspecting family members. The instruments of choice include the piano, guitar, violin, cello, flute, and clarinet (drums are usually a no-no). The Baby BAP continues to pursue her musical talents until it is clear her talents lie elsewhere.

Dance

After a few dance lessons, Baby BAP's goal of debuting in *The Nutcracker* and joining the Alvin Ailey dance troupe is all-consuming.

Mom and Dad just want her to develop some grace so she doesn't end up a clumsy oaf. Who started the rumor that all Black people have rhythm? While some Baby BAPs are hams who show off at their dance recitals, others just don't get it. These rhythmically challenged BAPs are known to *rélévé* as their fellow dancers *plié*. They become hopelessly frustrated as Madame Trotsky tells them to tuck in their ample African derrieres. Even if Baby BAP can't dance a lick, that doesn't mean she's not a prima donna.

Tennis

Tennis, the original BAPsport . . . is the sport for life. Who says there's no love in tennis? Just take a peek in your local racquet club and you'll find Baby BAPs prancing about on the tennis court. Actually, it's a family affair—it's easy for Baby BAP to take lessons while Mom's enjoying hers. As certain as balls bounce, the BAP knows how to hold her own on the court. No . . . she may not be the next Venus Williams, but she will be able to finesse the ball over the net. Through countless lessons, Baby BAPs learn the sport that they will carry with them for the rest of their lives.

Skiing

Don't believe the hype; Black folks can ski. It's not so rare these days to observe BAP toddlers hitting the blues and greens. Slowly but surely the next Cheryl Swoopes of the slopes is being molded. Sure, she has the form of a pro. And naturally, the Baby BAP bunny has to have her Polo Sport sweater and pants, K2 skis, Salomon bindings and boots.

The chalet set is so dazzled by her fabulous attire, they hardly notice when she wipes out.

Swimming

Reflecting on her diverse background, the Baby BAP is as well versed in the Australian crawl as she is in French. As a member of a highly active and social family unit, she can expect to spend an inordinate amount of time in and around water. From the backyard pool to Caribbean beaches, Baby BAP has a natural affinity for the water. Swimming may keep Baby BAP fit, but it is treacherous on her hair. One second in the water means that her kinks multiply exponentially. Sure, she loves the water, but dealing with her hair can be too much (she eventually tires of the breaststroke—a hair saver!). As she gets older she usually turns to other sports so she doesn't have to deal with her hair so much. (There's a reason Spelman doesn't have a pool!)

Social Calendar: Pencil Me In

While finishing schools may be formally kaput, in the BAP universe they flourish. The finest of them all is Jack and Jill of America, Inc. Oh, there are many pretenders to the throne . . . Tots 'n Teens, and Trees and Twigs . . . but Jack and Jill is the alpha and omega of the BAP set. Jack and Jill, a veritable Who's Who of Black America, is a country club without walls. Membership is exclusive, activities plentiful, and BAP mothers secretly use their inside advantage to plan their daughters' weddings. Sure it's an elitist organization, but these are just ordinary elitist folks who want the best for their offspring!

Is it so snobby to ride horseback, go to museums, or attend the theater with people who share the same background, bank accounts, and set of values? Of course it is. They aren't called Black American Princesses for nothing!

Top Eight Reasons a BAP Joins Jack and Jill

8. She's too young to choose her own friends.
7. To expose her to the "Art of Do-Gooding" (believe it or not, Jack and Jill members must complete one public service activity every year).
6. So she won't be the only Black child at her birthday party.
5. So her parents don't feel guilty about sending her to a predominantly white school.
4. So she does not forget she is Black.
3. Network. Network. Network (with Black people).
2. Pipeline to marriage (to a Black man).
1. Par-tay.

October

SUNDAY	MONDAY	TUESDAY
	1 4:00–6:00 Gymnastics	**2** 3:00–5:00 Tennis
7 11:00 Church 2:00 Visit Grandmommy and Granddaddy	**8** 4:00–6:00 Brownies Playdate at Camile's house	**9** 3:00–5:00 Tennis
14 11:00 Church 2:00 Ringling Brother, Barnum & Bailey's Circus	**15** 4:00–6:00 Gymnastics	**16** 3:00–5:00 Tennis Wendy comes over to play after Tennis
21 11:00 Church 2:00 Visit Grandmommy and Granddaddy	**22** 4:00–6:00 Brownies 7:00–9:00 Family Night at the Field Museum of Natural History	**23** 3:00–5:00 Tennis
28 11:00 Church 3:00 Ice Skating at new indoor rink	**29** 4:00–6:00 Gymnastics	**30** 3:00–5:00 Tennis Help Mommy make cupcakes

WEDNESDAY	THURSDAY	FRIDAY	SATURDAY
3 4:00–5:00 Piano Lesson	**4** 4:00–6:30 Swim team practice	**5** 4:00–5:00 Ballet Lesson 8:00 Alvin Ailey with Mommy and Daddy	**6** 11:00–3:00 Karen's birthday party—Splash party at Knoll Hill Country Club 4:00 Hair Appointment
10 4:00–5:00 Piano Lesson 7:00–8:00 French Tutor	**11** 4:00–6:30 Swim team practice	**12** 4:00–5:00 Ballet Lesson 6:00 Kelly sleeps over;rent videos; order pizza	**13** 1:00 Jack and Jill Monthly Activity-Horseback riding
17 4:00–5:00 Piano Lesson	**18** 4:00–6:30 Swim team practice	**19** 4:00–5:00 Ballet Lesson 7:00 Movies with Daddy	**20** 10:00 Visit Women's shelter with Mommy to help people 4:00 Hair Appointment
24 4:00–5:00 Piano Lesson 7:00–8:00 French Tutor	**25** 4:00–6:30 Swim team practice	**26** 4:00–5:00 Ballet Lesson 7:00 Sleepover at Kendell's house	**27** Shopping with Mommy 8:00 Go to see play with Mommy and Daddy
31 Class Haloween Party—Take cupcakes and costume 6:00 Trick or Treating			

A Day in the Life

A Butterfly Day—Age Eight

6:45 A.M.	Wake up and get dressed for school (if Mom's busy, hair sometimes looks a little crazy, due to my inadequate self-braiding technique).
7:30 A.M.	Catch the crosstown bus to Martin Luther King Elementary School for Science and Mathematics (read book-club book for after-school latchkey reading group—kids have reading clubs, too!).
8:30 A.M.	School begins—favorite class is Science (I want to be a scientist someday, I aspire to be like Madame Curie). Spelling. Social studies. Math. English. Spanish. Gym.
3:00 P.M.	Brownie troop meeting.
4:00 P.M.	Catch the crosstown bus home and think of "yo' mama" jokes so that I can beat LaQuita at the dozens tonight.
5:00 P.M.	Help Mom make dinner and eat with the family.
6:00 P.M.	Play outside until the streetlights come up (good time to catch up on gossip I missed while across town at MLK S&M).
7:00 P.M.	Go inside and finish homework.
8:00 P.M.	Watch Nickelodeon.
9:00 P.M.	Bedtime.

A Boho Day—Age Ten

6:45 A.M.	Wake up.
6:50 A.M.	Go back to sleep.
6:51 A.M.	Mom entices me from bed with croissants and jam.
7:00 A.M.	Argue with sisters about who has first dibs on the bathroom, then shower and brush teeth.
7:12 A.M.	Put away clothes Mom picked out for me—get favorite pants with Chinese silk trim on the cuffs.
7:15 A.M.	Argue with Mom about pants.
7:17 A.M.	Reluctantly put on what Mom already picked out for me.
7:30 A.M.	Our chauffeur, Wardell, arrives to drive us to school.
8:00 A.M.–3:00 P.M.	
	Geography—one of my favorite classes.
	French—*je vais au Paris dans le printemps, j'espérè!*
	Math—math + me = bored!
	Phys-Ed—square dancing, yuck!
	Art—we are doing ceramics, I'm making a little pitcher for Mom.
	Physical science—we're dissecting a grasshopper next week—wow!
4:00 P.M.–5:30 P.M.	Horseback Riding Lessons English Style. I hope I get my own saddle for Christmas.
6:00 P.M.–7:00 P.M.	Dinner with Mom and Dad and my two irritating older sisters.
7:00 P.M.–9:00 P.M.	Homework.

| 9:30 P.M. | Bed. |
| 9:30 P.M. | Finish writing short stories under my covers. |

A Bogus Day—Age Twelve

7:00 A.M.	Alarm sounds programmed with my favorite song: "Simply the Best" by Tina Turner.
7:01 A.M.	Mom tells me to get up and informs me that I'll have to walk to school this morning because she's got to get to work early today.
7:08 A.M.	Snooze.
7:16 A.M.	Snooze.
7:24 A.M.	Snooze.
7:32 A.M.	Snooze.
7:40 A.M.	Realize I'm going to be late.
7:41 A.M.	Jump in shower.
7:50 A.M.	Get dressed; put on some of Mom's makeup.
8:00 A.M.	Race out the door with Pop Tarts in hand.
8:20 A.M.	Sent to headmaster's office for late pass to homeroom.
8:25 A.M.	Make up excuse for being late. "I tripped over a rock and ripped my skirt so I had to go back and change."

8:30 A.M.	Roll eyes during lecture on the importance of being on time; followed by phone call to Mom by the secretary re: tardiness.
9:00 A.M.–11:45 A.M.	Math, English, and Spanish (get caught passing notes in Spanish class).
11:45 A.M.–12:00 noon	Scolded by Spanish teacher and given a detention.
12:00 noon–12:40 P.M.	Lunch—Preside over a mini-seminar for my "girls." Discussions include topics such as "How to cut class and go shopping," "What to wear tomorrow," "The art of French kissing," and "How to get out of homeroom."
12:45 P.M.–3:20 P.M.	Art, Health Sciences, and PE (before PE I got caught in the utility closet making out with James, one of my "girls'" boyfriends).
3:20 P.M.	School ends—hang out to watch James play basketball.

4:30 P.M.	Head home 'cuz I realized James will be walking Pam home.
4:50 P.M.	Arrive home; turn on TV.
5:00 P.M.–7:00 P.M.	Start homework—talk on the phone between math problems.
7:00 P.M.	Mom arrives with dinner and lecture about my misbehavior.
7:40 P.M.	Throw temper tantrum; go to room and slam door.
7:45 P.M.	Mom grounds me for two weeks.
7:50 P.M.	Sweet talk Mom out of the two week grounding.
8:00 P.M.	Get ready for bed, finish homework.
9:00 P.M.	Sneak phone under covers to call James and talk until 9:30 P.M. when Mom picks up phone.

A Betty Day—Age Sixteen

6:25 A.M.	Prepare to face the day by thinking happy, uplifting thoughts.
6:40 A.M.	Get out of bed; head to the bathroom to start my beauty regimen.
7:20 A.M.	Look at the outfit I picked out last night and smile to myself 'cuz I'm going to look fabulous!
7:30 A.M.	BAP hair . . . slight adjustment required: curl one, bump two. Finish look with lipstick.
8:00 A.M.	School starts. Physics. Dance. Trig. French II.
12:00 noon	Lunch. Study for World History exam. Meet with African Sisters, Inc. sponsor to plan Spring fashion show. I'm the VP.
1:00 P.M.	World History. English Lit. Free Period.

3:00 P.M.	Talk to English Lit. teacher . . . finish research paper due in two weeks; convince her to review paper now so it doesn't get lost in the sea of rough drafts she'll receive from other students.
3:30 P.M.	Home. Afternoon snack . . . critical to maintain energy level (treat self ☺). Watch *Cosby Show* reruns. Play with Penny the poodle: walk her, time permitting.

4:00 P.M.	Homework. Homework. Homework. Check out planner to prioritize.
4:30 P.M.	Erica calls. Ask her to call back after 9:30 P.M. once I've finished my homework.
7:00 P.M.	Run errands—return movies, run to the drug store.
8:00 P.M.	Dinner. Mommy cooked (I don't know how to cook yet).
8:30 P.M.	Read for pleasure. I take pride in finishing at least one book a week.
9:30 P.M.	Phone time. Lounge time.
10:30 P.M.	Lights out. I get grumpy if I don't get a full night's rest.

"Operation Getting Over"—Annual Summer Conventions

Like a gaggle of geese, the families of Black professionals make their annual trek to designated cities to hobnob at the National Medical, Dental, or Bar Association, the Boule, or Links conventions. Formed decades ago in response to being rejected by white organizations, the conventions sponsored by these organizations provide networking and educational opportunities for its members. But ask any BAP attendee what these conventions are all about and she'd respond with one word—"partying."

While her parents attend meetings and socialize with old friends, BAPgirl institutes "Operation Getting Over." Her main objective: To get away with anything and everything! She convinces her superiors, in order to ensure maximum intellectual exposure, that she must move up an age group and have her curfew extended. The true goal: to hang out with the older kids, find the "hospitality suite" (the room of the kid who is the ultimate master of "Operation Getting Over"), find a love-interest to tell her friends at home about, and to find at least one new pen pal.

These annual conventions validate BAPgirl and her way of life. For at least seven days out of each year, BAPgirl is surrounded by children who are just like her. With this group of kids she doesn't have to worry about answering questions about "talking white," her hair, or downplaying her family's success. She just plain fits in.

Before one convention ends, everyone, kids and parents alike, is talking excitedly about the next one. These annual conventions provide a much needed social outlet for the families they serve; long-lasting friendships are made and rekindled each year.

Letter Writing

The BAPgirl collects friends like she collects shoes, from only the finest places—summer camp, annual professional conventions, and Jack and

Jill Teen Regionals: BAPgirl's parents encourage her to keep in touch with the friends she meets. When she's old enough to travel alone, BAPgirl visits her friends and their families on a regular basis. During the school year the best way to keep in touch is by writing letters.

Letter writing takes precedence over phone calls and e-mails due, in large part, to BAPgirl's hectic schedule. Well trained, she can always find time to jot a note in between classes, after school lessons, or before bed. Letter writing is a fine art, and as such, requires the appropriate canvas. Personalized stationery from Tiffany & Co., Cranes, or Dempsey & Carroll is for more formal writing (you know, for the obligatory thank you notes). But funky personalized stationery is for those all-important BAPgirl secrets. BAParents don't mind this indulgence because their princesses are increasing their vocabularies and honing their writing skills.

Take Her Out to the Ball Game . . .

If you take her out to the ball game, she might become interested in sports . . .

The BAP becomes more self-disciplined, confident, and independent if she plays sports. If you don't let her play sports, she'll turn into your worst nightmare, a petulant prissy.

A content BAP is a busy BAP, engaging in at least two sports a year. Even participating in three isn't uncommon—this is all in preparation for her Maalox moment.

If you take her out to the ball game, she will step up to the plate . . .

She will carry her fashion awareness to the playing field. Her sporting attire will make her the envy of all her competitors. If it is the latest shoe, skirt, or warmup, BAPgirl will wear it well. It's all about being the best—in her world it's not who wins or loses, but how good she looks when she stomps her opponent.

If you take her out to the ball game, she will hit a home run on the playing field and in the classroom . . .

Her grades won't drop because her busy schedule will foster disciplined study habits.

If you take her out to the ball game . . .

She will experience the thrill of victory and the agony of defeat. She will participate in athletic activities forever. She will continue playing the sport of her formative years or take up new challenges. No couch potatoes here!

BAPgirl in Sports

BAPgirl cannot imagine that girls were once relegated to the sidelines. Who says a Black woman can't win Wimbledon? Althea Gibson and Venus would be appalled. Who says that the BAP's butt will throw off her beam routine? Give gold medalist Dominique Dawes a call. Who says no Black woman would ever medal in figure skating? Look in the history books for Debi Thomas. If you let her play sports . . . there's no limit to what BAPgirl can do.

Golf

Daddy is typically the first to introduce his daughter to golf. As a youngster, BAPgirl enjoys chauffeured rides in the golf cart and occasional trips to the driving range. It is a special treat when Daddy lets her hit a ball or two. Even better is when Daddy purchases a set of clubs for his little one. Although BAPgirl is exposed to golf at an early age, it is not until she matures that she learns to truly appreciate the sport (but what other sport can she play and find such fine young men like Tiger Woods?).

Ice Skating

Since being a prima donna is in her blood, it is only natural that BAPgirl learns to ice skate. What little girl can resist the lure of being the center of attention? Captivated by the images of Dorothy Hamill, Debi Thomas, Surya Bonaly, and Michelle Kwan (to name a few), BAPgirl soon strong-arms her mother into footing the bill for lessons, skates, and the requisite adorable outfits. However, the "romanticism" of becoming a figure skater does not always last. It may wane after countless early morning practices, lost sleep, and a sore rear take their collective toll.

Soccer

Annually, over 2.5 million players age five through nineteen play soccer—the "Game for Kids." BAPgirls eagerly and enthusiastically contribute to this number. Soccer helps BAPgirls to understand the importance of teamwork. As with other BAPgirl sports, soccer promotes good sportsmanship and instills self-confidence through participation and accomplishment.

Gymnastics

Her floor routine begins with tumbling in nursery school and the domestic trampoline (her parents' bed). Fed up with BAPgirl's living room antics, Mom enrolls her in gymnastics to spare the furniture. In no time, round-offs, handsprings, and "aerials" become second nature to BAPgirl.

Field Hockey

Field hockey is and has always been a sport for sadists, and BAPgirls are no exception. As one of the world's most popular sports, the preppy variety of BAPgirl is never one to pass up an opportunity to look exceptionally cute. BAPgirls like field hockey because they get to wear sassy little kilts while putting the big hurt on the crosstown archrival. Only lacrosse players share in this unique joy of wearing skirts while being daredevils on the field. However, if BAPgirl wants to keep her teeth or shins intact, this isn't the sport for her.

Lacrosse

Lacrosse, originally a Native American sport played to the death, was co-opted by the private school set. Of course, everyone thinks she's crazy for playing a sport which combines the savagery of the NHL with the WASPiness of the bluest of blue bloods. But a BAPgirl is never one to let tradition stand in the way.

Equestrian

What is it about a little girl and her love of horses? The BAPgirl falls in love with horses as a small child. For her birthday and Christmas she tells her parents she wants a horse. Her parents indulge her fantasy, showering her with plush stuffed-animal horses, books, and even riding lessons. While appreciative, she remains relentless in her pursuit. She wants a horse and won't rest until she has one. Finally, her parents succumb. BAPgirl is successful once again.

Brains Are Good and So Are Books, but People Judge You by Your Looks

It's not often that one finds a baby who has a good fashion sense. The BAP infant arrives home from the hospital swaddled in a Neiman Marcus blanket, and upchucks on her funky Baby Gap outfits. Later, she crawls about in the best jumpers and Florence Eiseman dresses. When BAPgirl outgrows her Peter Rabbit Wedgwood, so begins a lifetime of shopping. BAPgirl's introduction to shopping begins at Saks Fifth Avenue for Back to School and Spring Forward shopping. At first she doesn't quite understand the concept and even finds it loathsome. She likens accompanying her mother on shopping sprees to waiting for the guillotine. A whole Saturday is spent lying on the floors of dressing rooms, toting heavy shopping bags around, and dealing with pushy salespeople—ugh!! The BAPgirl has visions of Barbies dancing in her head.

As she matures, shopping isn't the dreaded exercise it used to be. It becomes fun as salespeople treat her like a queen for the day. The nightmare suddenly transforms into a mother-daughter bonding experience. When she arrives home with her stash, BAPgirl models her clothes for Daddy, but only after she meticulously removes all of the price tags (there's no need to send Daddy into premature cardiac arrest, the arrival of the bills will be sufficient).

Once Mommy decides that her princess is old enough to shop for her own clothes, BAPgirl is authorized to use her parents' credit cards at Saks, Neiman's, and Bloomies. What was once a biannual event becomes at minimum a quarterly foray into the racks. Appearance, she's learned through her shopping excursions with Mommy, is of the utmost importance!

The BAP Incentive Program

It starts out innocently enough . . . the BAPgirl sees something she must have and her mother says she'll buy it for her as a reward if she keeps her room clean for a week, stops biting her fingernails, gets along with her sibling[s], and so on. BAPgirl knows a challenge when she sees one and meets her mother's request head-on. The new shirt, umbrella, purse, jeans, tennis shoes, or CD is hers once she tackles her demon!

This little "incentive" program BAP mothers employ has interesting long-lasting effects. Right or wrong, it teaches BAPgirl that "good behavior" will always be rewarded—preferably with fabulous things. In addition, it instills positive traits like the Four P's! (Remember? Precision, Perfection, Patience, and Persistence.) While the parental program may expire after college, fret not! BAPs proudly continue the tradition of treating themselves for a job well done!

Dear Diary,

Mommy, Hillary and I just got back from "Back to School" shopping. I'm beginning to like this shopping thing. It seems like every year Mommy buys more and more clothes for me. I can't wait until Daddy comes home so that Hillary and I can put on a fashion show for him. You know what was totally cool about shopping this year? Mommy bought me my first Louis Vuitton bag. Can you believe it? My very own. She also said that if I continue to get good grades she might buy me another one.

Summer vacation is almost over. I had soooo much fun this year. I went back to overnight camp. This time I could only stay for two weeks because I'm playing in more tennis tournaments. Guess what? When I qualified for the Westerns Mommy and Daddy bought me the rollerblades I've been dying to have... just for winning the tournament. I saw Leslie and Rebecca at the NMA convention. I hope they can come and visit me before the end of summer. Last week we got back from Jamaica; I love it down there. I get to swim all day, go horseback riding, and play tennis. It's so much fun!

Well, I have to go. Bye for now!
Betty Betty

P.S. Sometimes I think Mommy is weird. Today, she told me that whenever I have an extra credit project at school this year I have to do it on something related to Black people. I wonder why?

BAPgirl Rules

"The Rules" are not just for the marriage-minded. BAPgirls have a set of their own to abide by:

DO

- Get braces—they're *de rigueur*.
- Whine until you get a car for your sweet sixteen.
- Throw a sweet sixteen to rival the Royal Wedding.
- Have a minimum one-month supply of clothing in your closet.
- Have a standing hair appointment by the age of ten.
- Visit the dermatologist regularly to have a beautiful complexion like Halle Berry's.
- Make sure you're an authorized user of parental credit cards.
- Wear pearl studs—it's a rite of passage.

DON'T

- Show out in public.
- Do the dirty deed before college—Mom can always tell.
- Kiss on the first date—you have the BAP image to uphold.
- Tell Daddy how much money Mommy spent on your clothes.
- Wear the same thing twice—even if others don't remember, your subconscious will!
- Date a boy whose pants defy gravity, whose hair is longer than yours, or who wears more jewelry than you.
- Leave the house in rollers and slippers—that's, well, we all know what that is . . . it's G-H-E-T-T-O!

Hot Fun in the Summertime

When the March winds give way to the dog days of summer, parents breathe a collective sigh of relief before reality hits—"What to do with my little BAP?!?" This is a slight exaggeration, of course, because any parent worth more than their weight in a Range Rover would have already planned the young BAP's summer activities during late winter or early spring. While some view summer vacation as a time to let off some steam and relax, BAParents use the summer to overload their daughter's already full agenda.

If BAPgirl attends a predominantly white school and does not have the opportunity to socialize with other BAPgirls, summer camp is a perfect occasion to broaden her cultural horizons. The oldest and most well-known Black camp is Camp Atwater in North Brookfield, Massachusetts.

Just Because You're at Camp with Little White Girls. . . .

- Doesn't mean you can wash and blow-dry your hair every day.
- Doesn't mean you're the ambassador for the Black race.
- Doesn't mean that the counselors should do your hair.
- It, especially, doesn't mean that you are one!

Summer Activities for High Schoolers

Camp is not every young BAP's cup of Earl Grey. The high school BAP may feel it is a juvenile pursuit and prefer to spend her time intensifying her studies for college. Who knows, she might meet a studious but cool young man to boot. Summertime presents an opportunity to explore an interest like marine biology, English literature, or pre-med studies.

Attending a prestigious institution like Miss Porter's Summer Challenge or the Wellesley College Exploration Program also expands the young BAP's purview and gives her a chance to test the college experience. Listed below are several enrichment programs for a variety of interests.

INROADS, Inc.
Wellesley College Exploration Program
Miss Porter's Summer Challenge
Summer Abroad Programs
Oxbridge Academic Programs
People to People Student Ambassador Programs
Children's International Summer Villages

Summer's Almost Over . . . Where Are You Going?

1. Caribbean
2. Europe
3. The Disneys
4. Cruises
5. New York City
6. Martha's Vineyard
7. Down South
8. Africa

A Four-Letter Word

Work? . . . Some say it's never too soon too learn the value of a dollar, but in the BAP's case the longer she waits, the more detrimental it is. Some BAParents learn this lesson the hard way. Camp and summer school were not options for Willow—she'd had her fill of them. Spending the summer by the pool was all she really wanted to do. "Get a job," however, is what her BAParents told her. Her imploring "whys" were answered with, "So you can learn the value of a dollar and stop spending money like it grows on trees!" "The value of a dollar?" she said. "I know the value of a dollar. I know that working for minimum wage at some store or boutique is not worth the gas it would take for me to get there." Agreeing that she was right and obviously knew more about money than they'd given her credit for, Willow spent a relaxing summer lounging by the pool.

Dear Diary,

Well—I've memorized the Frommer's guide to Paris from front to back. Ask me anything about Paris and I won't fail in describing it. I mean that was my summer vacation—that doesn't mean everyone else has to know I traveled through my head. My aunt has a fabulous apartment on the Champs Elysées—she's been living there for years. She took me everywhere—I even went to a restaurant and ate escargot. We traveled to the South of France where all the beautiful people are—we fit right in. My Aunt Carmelita is tray chic—she bought me a ton of clothes while I was there but my luggage was stolen on the way back home. It was a wonderful trip—I can't wait to tell everyone about it—especially those Jack and Jill types who are always doing such exciting things.

Chow.
Barbara Bogus

Twice as Good . . . The High School Years

The BAPgirl knows that she must be twice as good as her competitors in order to succeed. Others may scoff at her abilities, but she is driven to show them otherwise. As she comes into her own, the maddening crowds no longer inspire her as she looks to the ultimate competitor—herself.

Clubland

BAPgirl must stand out from the crowd. That's why her million-watt smile beams out from every page in the yearbook: Black Students' Association, *The Daily Trumpet,* debate team—you name it, she's there. She's the president, editor-in-chief, and BWOC (big woman on campus). It's a tough job, but someone has to do it.

BAPgirl breathes life into every club to which she belongs. She's the spark in French Club who volunteers her mother's quiche-making abilities for Le Bake Sale. She's the editor of the yearbook who devotes fifty pages to her closest friends. She's the student government president who assures the principal that the dance will end at midnight. She's the Black Students' Association member who builds the bridge between her Black and white friends.

Drama

Theatrics make up a part of any BAPgirl's life. Producing tears on cue or a smile that will illuminate a room is the result of some inborn talent. Unfortunately, BAPgirls involved in drama get a bad rap. It's true that they may be found cavorting in the cafeteria with fellow drama club members, speaking in absurd accents, and wearing scarves around their necks. They are irritating! But they are merely expressing their uninhibited nature, finding their voice in the wilderness of a stifling and confined, straight-laced high school.

Billie Boho

French Club President; Amnesty International campus Cofounder; Lacrosse Team Captain; Drama Club—directed *Raisin in the Sun* and *The Glass Menagerie*; Forensics; member of PETA.

Barbara Bogus

Fashion Club Founder; Future Shoppers of America; Students for Fur Coats and Accessories; Cheerleader, 9th grade through 12th grade.

Betty Betty

Student Government President, 12th grade; Model U.N. Secretary General; Tennis Team Varsity Captain, 11th and 12th grade; Tennis Team J.V. Captain, 9th and 10th grade; Vice President, Future Leaders of America; Links debutante.

Bonita Butterfly

Pre-Med Society; Oprah's Book Club; President—Future Leaders of America.

Cheerleading

Cheerleading requires several qualities: first agility, to jump higher to see that cute boy in the stands; second, creativity, to make your out-fit stand out from the rest; and finally, a perky personality (the better to charm with, my dear). It's no secret that cheerleading BAPgirls have two things in mind: exercise and meeting boys.

Dear Maude and Tommy (just kidding—Hi Mom and Dad),

Having a great time as usual at Interlochen. My harp lessons are going well, except I don't know where they'll lead me.... Mom, do I really have to be in the cotillion when I get back home? It is so yuck! Those stupid big dresses and curtseys, it's so not me. Dad, I hope I can still go to the NDA this year—all of my friends are go-ing ... no, I'm not too old to go!

Well, see you in four weeks (send $$, please).

Love,

Billie Boho

P.S. Okay, I quit the harp. I'm playing drums in an all-girl, all-Black band called Rosa's Revenge (in tribute to Rosa Parks). I'll need a new set of Pearl drums with Zildjian cymbals and a hi-hat.

Sweet Sixteen

Sweet Sixteen Party Recipe
2c raging hormones
$1/2$ tsp good sense
a sprinkle of boys
a sprinkle of girls
Stir ingredients quickly as they will go out of control rapidly. Pour into fly party gear. Let sit in a country club or hotel ballroom for 4–5 hours. And, voilà, you have the perfect BAP sweet sixteen.

Debs—The Debutante Balls

Oh to be a deb! Besides her first recital, sweet sixteen, first date, college graduation, and wedding . . . the BAP's debut into society is another Broadway production. Being a deb is a given, it's a rite of passage for BAPgirls. The transition from childhood to adulthood is marked by a debutante ball, also known as a big bash! Annually, hundreds of BAPgirls are presented to society in cotillions sponsored by private organizations like The Links, Inc., Alpha Kappa Alpha Sorority, Inc., and Delta Sigma Theta Sorority, Inc.

The process of becoming a debutante is an exhausting one! From the selection process to her deep curtsey before hundreds, BAPgirl endures an intense year of preparation.

1. The Nomination. Approximately one year prior to the cotillion, members from the sponsoring organizations collect the names of prospective debs. Each potential debutante must have a sponsoring organization member attest to her good character.

Next, BAPgirl is required to attend an informational tea where she demonstrates her social graces to members of the sponsoring organization. This is easy for BAPgirl because many members of the sponsoring organization are Mommy's friends. The tea is nothing more than another event with Mommy and her friends who brag about their daughters' accomplishments.

2. The Invitation. After the tea, the debutante committee invites BAPgirl to apply for the ball. If BAPgirl has the "right" parents, an invitation is guaranteed. A well-kept secret, the selection process is all about who you know.

3. The Escort. Once accepted as a debutante, each BAPgirl must recruit a young gentleman as an escort. The ideal escort candidate should be handsome, charming, coordinated, and, of course, come from a "good family" (boyfriends don't necessarily make the best escorts because their longevity isn't guaranteed). Brothers, cousins, and good family friends are often forced to serve as escorts. All escorts must be approved by the sponsoring organization.

4. The Preparation. Starting in February of BAPgirl's senior year, the debutantes meet as a group for the first time. At this meeting the debutantes are informed that every Sunday afternoon until the night of the ball will be consumed with cotillion activities. Also, some balls require that debs perform a community service activity or raise money. In these instances, the debutante who raises the most money receives special recognition. During the first month, debutantes attend workshops on everything from fashion to etiquette. The next two and one-half months are spent with the choreographer. The debutantes and escorts learn various waltzes, a minuet, the tango, and many other ballroom dances. The escorts practice dancing with the BAPmoms and the debs practice waltzing with their first prince charming—Daddy.

5. The Dress. The cotillion is one event where BAPgirl shines like never before. Tradition requires that she wear a white floor-length dress, white kid gloves, white shoes, and pearls. Individuality is paramount. Can you imagine if two debs showed up wearing the same dress? What a travesty! To prevent this horrifying possibility, many BAPgirls have their gowns custom-made or head to the formal dress department at Neiman's or Saks.

6. The Ball. The process that commenced a year ago culminates in a gala production. On the special night, the debutantes are presented by their fathers to the assembly. As BAPgirl curtseys, her biography is read and flashbulbs from the local society pages go off like search-lights. The escorts collectively hold their breath while they anxiously wait for their partners to make their way down the runway. After the last deb is presented, the debs dance with their fathers, and then the fun begins. The escorts and debs show off the elaborate dances they've practiced over the past months. The evening ends with an an-nouncement about the debutantes' fund-raising efforts. The deb who raises the most money leads the other debutantes, the escorts, and the parents in the grand finale march.

BAP Quiz #2

Just to make sure you've been paying attention. . . .

The Look is what BAPmoms give when
    a. The BAP needs to calm down
    b. She's working her mom's last nerve
    c. She is about to get her bottom smacked
    d. All of the above

Boho's first summer job is at
    a. McDonald's
    b. Tiffany & Co.
    c. At her mother or father's office
    d. She can't work in the summer, she spends it on the Vineyard

Butterflies typically wear
   a. Retail designer wear
   b. Wholesale designer wear
   c. Outlet mall designer wear
   d. Whatever their mothers tell them to wear

Bettys have
   a. A standing weekly appointment to have their three-inch nails airbrushed
   b. Several pairs of Birkenstocks
   c. A modest background
   d. A personal shopper by the age of ten

Boguses prefer to eat
   a. Lobster thermidor
   b. Lamb chops with mint sauce
   c. Veal in a raspberry-lime reduction
   d. Pickled pigs feet

Answer Key:
d. for all.

TO GO TO COLLEGE OR NOT TO GO TO COLLEGE? THIS IS *NOT* A QUESTION FOR THE BAP

hat did the BAP who did not go to college say to the BAP who did?

Hi. Welcome to McDonald's. May I take your order?

As open-minded as the BAP's parents pretend to be, when it comes to their daughter attending college they are about as liberal as Clarence Thomas. Their unanimous vote results in a two-pronged decision: 1. You have a choice, and here it is. 2. Go to college, or move out. The college application process is a breeze for BAPgirl. She's a star in the classroom; maven of the after-school set, and with the help of Stanley Kaplan she aces her SATs. All BAPgirl has to decide is what college she'll grace with her presence.

Does she go to her parents' alma mater? A Historically Black College or University (HBCU)? Ivy League? Seven Sisters? Big Ten? Small liberal arts?

Academic reputation, social life, and career options are the key factors in the decision-making process. The most notable event in the process is the old-fashioned college visit. Hands down, nothing else beats a homecoming at a Historically Black College. What teenager wouldn't be dazzled by the sights, sounds, and smells of step shows, marching bands, and soul food? But pre-freshman weekends at other universities and colleges put on good shows for BAPgirl and give HBCUs a run for their money. In the end, BAPgirl knows that she is meant for the best life has to offer as she heads off to her college of choice. As usual, she chooses the "Best and Nothing Less."

Freedom, Friendship, and Fun

Four years of freedom, friendship, and fun is what college is all about. Freedom to sleep in, skip class, watch soaps, or drink rum and Coke. Lifelong friendships are formed in 12×12 rooms, where deep secrets are shared and relationships critically analyzed. Fun is doing whatever she wants, whenever she wants with whomever she wants. This may even mean learning the steps to the "horizontal mambo." But just in case the BAP strays too far afield, there's always . . .

Pre-Collegiate Maternal Admonitions

1. Remember you are in college to get an education
2. Find a church home
3. Call home on Sundays
4. Don't sit on the toilet
5. Wear a scarf when you go to sleep
6. Always wear your shower shoes

7. Don't bring home any babies
8. Find a husband

Dorm Room Essentials

BAP	Bogus
Compact stereo	Bose Surround Sound system
Ralph Lauren sheets	50/50 poly-cotton blend
13-inch color TV	Anything larger than 13-inch
Pentium computer	Pentium desktop and laptop

Instant Message
From: billie.boho@Spelmanfirstyear.edu
To: atate@wesleyan.edu
Subject: College Life

Hey there! Are you all moved in? I am. I think my dad may have gotten a hernia dragging my trunk up three flights of stairs. He reminded me that there was no need to bring my entire library. My room, expressive and eclectic, really captures my budding negritude (vocab word from Afro 101 syllabus). I did get several new sets of Ralph Lauren sheets—I can't seem to sleep on anything else. You should come down for Morehouse's Homecoming. Peace and Love, Billie Boho

The BAP tells her parents she's majoring in. . . .	They tell her. . . .
Black Studies	It took eighteen years for you to figure out you're Black?
Physical Education	Who's paying your tuition next semester?
Art History	I hope they teach you the history of the paycheck.

French   *Pourquoi?*

Economics   That's our girl!

Instant Message
From: bonitabutterfly@university.edu
To: Skeeboz@aol.com
Subject: hi

Hey girl . . . . how's the whole college thing working out for you? These professors are no joke! I feel like I'm constantly behind. How are you supposed to go to class, go to work, study, *and* hang out? I have to tell you, I met these girls here who make Whitley from *A Different World* seem tame in comparison. I knew there were black folks out there with money, I just never figured they'd be a part of my crowd or I a part of theirs. Can you believe I'm thinking about pledging? We'll have to save that for a phone call, you can never be sure who has access to your email! bb

House of BAP (College Couture)

Scoping out BAPs isn't too hard to do and the quad of any college campus is a great place to do just that. BAPs put the fear in fierce— their style and grace overwhelms the unwashed masses. Here are a few selections from the collegiate wardrobe.

FALL

Breakfast at Tiffany's   A 100 percent cotton man's dress shirt worn with drop earrings.

All My Soap Operas   For the fashionable femme, the latest wear for the TV lounge set

---

consists of an Aspen baseball cap, roomy linen shorts, and the ubiquitous white Tee.

WINTER

Classroom Queen

Studious—she's all business in her Tahari suit. Guess who has an interview after class?

SPRING

Spring Fling

When a young girl's fancy turns to showing some skin. Cute little tanks, baby Tees, and pants that tastefully accentuate the BAP's figure.

Pomp and Circumstance

While clothes make the man, it takes a BAP to make the clothes. Resplendent in her Cynthia Rowley dress, she throws on her cap and gown and wears them with equal flair.

Butterfly Fashion Faux Pas

1. Tacky rings on every finger.
2. Shellacking her baby hair to the sides of her face.
3. Upsweep hairdos plastered around foam.
4. Black pantyhose with anything other than black shoes.
5. Stirrup pants.

Hey Chica! I am missing that Cuban chicken from Versailles on La Cienega! How I wish I were back in LA! The people down here are just too conservative. When I wear my Mexican dress and Birkies to class—all I get are stares.

Be happy! You could live in the naked dorm like me. Oops, I'm not being p.c., I mean the clothing optional dorm. Talk about staring—yuck the bodies on some of these people. I see why clothes were invented!

BAP Colleges and Universities of Choice

The following are the top BAP schools. Except for the preeminent BAP college—Spelman College—the schools are presented in alphabetical order.

Spelman College
Atlanta, Ga.

BAPs from all corners of the world make their hajj to this BAP mecca. It doesn't hurt that Morehouse College is across the street.

Amherst College
Amherst, Mass.

For the outdoorsy BAP who wants to escape the hustle and bustle of urban life. And we do mean escape. Amherst is a three-hour drive from Beantown by car. Start learning how to whittle. Make friends with Smithies and Holyokers.

University of California at Berkeley
Berkeley, Cal.

Used to be for the radical '60s "dread set." Now a last choice due to Proposition 209. Fight the power.

Brown University
Providence, R.I.

The pass/fail system may lure the Ivy League BAP who likes to get her groove on. But if you party too hard, it's pass for them and fail for you.

Hampton University
Hampton, Va.

Cast your buckets down where you are because this school is in the boonies. For the BAP whose parents want her to graduate before the next millennium (see Howard).

Howard University
Washington, D.C.

The black hole . . . many go in, but few rarely come out (at least in four years). Think about it. How many people do you know who graduated from Howard on time?

New York University
New York, N.Y.

If you can make it here, you can make it anywhere. Temptation is everywhere. Any store on 57th Street, the funky bazaars on 8th Avenue, and don't forget SoHo. A shopper's paradise and student's nightmare. Oh yeah, the school is pretty good, too.

Northwestern University
Evanston, Ill.

The lake is its greatest attraction. Skinny-dipping, sunbathing, strolls under the moonlight. . . . Remember, it's warm in Chicago only a few months out of the year.

Oberlin College
Oberlin, Ohio

It's so crunchy you may crack a tooth. Located on the underground railroad, this school accepted Black people before slavery ended.

Princeton University
Princeton, N.J.

P stands for Princeton. *P* stands for preppy. *P* stands for pretentious. *P* stands for pretty popular with BAPs.

Stanford University
Palo Alto, Cal.

Palo Alto is beautiful. Stanford's campus is breathtaking. On campus there's a premium mall with Saks, Neiman's, and Banana Republic—what BAP could ask for anything more?

University of Michigan
Ann Arbor, Mich.
For BAPs who don't realize they should really be going East. It's a great school for homebodies who don't want to stray too far from their stomping grounds. Freshman year is like the thirteenth grade.

University of Pennsylvania
Philadelphia, Pa.
All of the ivy-ness, none of the stuffiness. This urban ivy-league institution attracts the budding BAP business mogul.

University of Virginia
Charlottesville, Va.
Founded by Thomas Jefferson. The father of our nation (and some Black folks, too). For the genteel, mint julep set.

Wellesley College
Wellesley, Mass.
The BAPpiest of the Seven Sisters. Betty and Boho would be most comfortable here, bloodline BAPs, rubbing shoulders with the bluest of the blue bloods.

Wesleyan University
Middletown, Conn.
Boho's stomping ground. Quiet as it's kept, Wesleyan turns out many artistic BAPs. Don't forget the reputedly clothing optional dorm.

Yale University
New Haven, Conn.
For the nerd in denial. Yalies know they're bright, but don't have to brag about it. Their biggest challenge . . . four years in New Haven.

The Top Ten Schools Where a BAP Can Get Her Mrs. Degree

1. Spelman/Morehouse College
2. Howard University
3. Harvard University
4. University of Pennsylvania
5. Stanford University
6. University of Virginia
7. Florida A&M University
8. Fisk University (Meharry Medical School is down the street!)
9. University of Michigan
10. Northwestern University

It's High Noon—Do You Know Where Your Groove Is?

A unique physio/sociological phenomenon occurs on college campuses across our great nation almost daily. The scientific name for such occurrences is *shakus groovethangus* (aka S.G.). It is primarily found at HBCUs and majority institutions that have a population of more than two Black students to rub together. At noon, S.G. takes over the student's mind with a quickness. S.G. is manifested by the victim's inability to focus on schoolwork or even attend class. The common side effects: unceasing music in head, foot-tapping, and breaking into a cold sweat when she sees a member of the opposite sex. Patients usually describe this feeling as a "move to groove." Institutions of higher learning have encouraged this bizarre behavior by allowing "lunchtime jams."

Young women who are casually dressed most of the week emerge on Fridays as if they stepped out of the pages of *Vogue.* Young men, prone to tipping Coke machines for sport, are on their best behavior. Add the appropriate hip-hop/trip-hop/acid jazz/r&b to the mix of frenzied postadolescents and you have *shakus groovethangus.*

How to Spot an Acute Case of S.G.

- When a parent calls his or her daughter at noon on Friday, her roommate swears she's studying and can't be disturbed.
- Your daughter's credit card (to be used only in emergencies) reveals a succession of "emergency" purchases at Bloomingdales or other retail stores, always on a Thursday.
- During Christmas break, every Friday you catch your daughter blasting music in the living room at noon—and dancing by herself.
- Your daughter has added subversive music to her collection.

S.G. Can Best Be Observed at. . . .

Spelman	Lower Manley Center and The Wall (on Clark's campus)
Howard	The Towers
University of Michigan	The Union
FAMU	The Set
Morehouse	Spelman College
Hampton	The Union, Cheers, and The Harbors
Northwestern	The Black House
Georgetown	Buffalo Billiards
University of Pennsylvania	Superblock and Dubois College House
Stanford	Ujamaa and The Black House
University of Illinois	The Union and The Quad

The Glamorous Life . . .

To pledge or not to pledge . . . as far as sororities are concerned, is the BAP's ultimate question. What *isn't* in question is which sorority the BAP will pledge. Zeta Phi Beta . . . no! Sigma Gamma Rho . . . why? The BAP knows that her platinum BAPcard™ is only valid in Alpha Kappa Alpha or Delta Sigma Theta sororities. (Okay, a few somehow managed to slip through the cracks when they joined the "other two," but they are forgiven.)

Before Betty and Boho leave for college, they hear countless stories of Greek life from Mommy and Daddy. Tales of dressing alike, walking "in line," big sisters or big brothers, and speaking in the first person plural for weeks on end are a part of the process. BAPs are told by their parents that pledging is grueling yet fulfilling. The BAP may make new friends and might meet a nice fraternity boy, all in the name of public service. Butterfly usually hasn't had the same exposure to sorority life. Once at school, Butterfly learns about pledging from her enlightened mentors, Betty and Boho. Don't forget about Bogus. Of course, she knows all there is to know about sororities. She even manages to finagle her way into one of the organizations. She never considers going GDI (God Damn Individual) because she mistakenly believes that "to pledge" is the only question. Little does Bogus know that simply because she's accepted in a sorority, she is not granted carte blanche access to BAPdom.

Instant Message
To: mrsbogus@aol.edu
From: sororbogus@justcrossed.edu
Subject: skee-wee

Hey Mom. I'm a full-fledged AKA now. The first and best sorority from which all others followed. I have sisters all around the world. It's pink and green from now to eternity. Getting into the Links and Jack and Jill will be a breeze!

Are You Ready to Throw Down?

The sounds from the party can be heard by those anxiously waiting to get in. Skeeeeee-wee. A FIΣ! Kay A Siggh. Ooooooooooooh oooop! Ruff-ruff. In circles around the dance floor, the different Greek organizations start calling out to one another. And so begins the night.

FRESHMAN YEAR. All eyes, male and female, are watching the women in the freshman class. Upper-class women observe the competition. Men check out the froshes—looking for love, looking to creep, and some just looking for the sake of looking. A warning to the naive newcomer . . . be careful of who you check out—he may belong to an upper-class sorority woman.

As much fun as they are, parties can be a source of confusion. Am I dressed appropriately? Does he like me? Do they know I want to pledge? Why are they so rude to me? . . . and the list goes on.

SOPHOMORE YEAR. Parties take on different meanings for different people. For the GDI, obviously a woman who marches to her own tune, she now has time to hang out and enjoy all that her BAP membership affords her (individuality, no worried phone calls from rushee sisters, and time to date!). For the neophytes, it's about being a part of the LIFE . . . steppin' around the parties, collecting money at the door, wearing paraphernalia, and calling out to her sorors. Then there's the poor, nervous rushee who has to impress the women who hold the key to her fate in the sorority. Heaven forbid that any attention she garnered as a freshman should be remembered! And please, let it be forgotten that she dated the dean of pledge's boyfriend in her freshman year.

JUNIOR YEAR. By now parties are becoming old hat . . . no longer considered "fresh meat," the junior women watch their male counterparts flirt shamelessly with freshmen. Parties are the last item on the GDI agenda now. She may go to one occasionally but prefers to hang with her friends or boyfriend. Last year's neophyte is this year's pro-phyte who now realizes she won't burn in hell for not wearing all of her paraphernalia at once. And the neophyte? She's in her glory, enjoying all the benefits of the LIFE.

SENIOR YEAR. Party? What party? Who's throwin' it? Can I get in for free?

Road Trippin'

Salsa—check. Blue corn tortillas—check. Good sounds—check. Good friends—check. A BAP won't hit the road without her handy-dandy AAA card (and Visa, AmEx, cash . . .). Whether it's homecoming or a short trip to visit friends at another school, it's all about letting loose for the weekend—and having fun.

Spring Vacation

"Go home for spring break? You're joking, right?"

Whether the BAP's off for a week to bask in the Caribbean sun or jetting away to hit the slopes one last time for the season, you can bet she has planned her trip to a T. She starts early as she puts in bids for the family vacation home or time-share. Before she knows it, spring break arrives and off she goes.

Popular Road Trips

1. Washington, D.C.—Howard University's homecoming
2. Atlanta, Ga.—Morehouse's homecoming
3. Philadelphia, Pa.—Penn Relays
4. Boston, Mass.—Head of the Charles
5. New Orleans, La.—Mardi Gras/The Bayou Classic
6. The Caribbean/Mexico—The Jazz Fests
7. Hilton Head—Spring Break
8. Palm Springs—Spring Break
9. South Beach Miami, Florida—Spring Break
10. Reggae ski week

Instant Message
From: BBOHO@alwaysbroke.com
To: DR.BOHO@deeppockets.net
Subject: Hola

___

Hey Dad! I found a cyber café in Cozumel! Can you believe it? Well you won't believe this. The ATM ate my card—could you send me a few pesos? Muchas gracias.
Billie

Reasons Why the BAP Simply Must Have a Car at College

1. I can't carry all of my shopping bags on the bus, now, can I?
2. Why not?
3. I'm on the dean's list, so I deserve one.
4. After a late night in science lab, I'm scared to walk across campus by myself.
5. Candy-apple red looks good with my complexion.

Maternal Admonitions—The Collegiate Years

1. Is that what you're wearing? (The old standard.)
2. I don't care how late you stay out when you're at school, you're under *my* roof now.
3. If you are not ready to go out this evening by nine, you're not leaving this house tonight.
4. If you can go out Saturday night, then you can get up and go to church on Sunday morning.
5. Sure, your boyfriend can come home with you for Thanksgiving. . . . Call your cousin Mike and see if he can stay there.
6. Don't think you're going to sit in this house all summer doing nothing!
7. You're not too big to spank.
8. This is still *my* house and you will do as I say.
9. I hope you have children just like you.

The Grad School–Bound BAP (The GBAP)

The BAP has taken just about every standardized test known to mankind . . . so why should she stop after college? After sixteen-plus years of tests, another one or two won't hurt, especially after Stanley Kaplan or Princeton Review shows her the way. Some BAPs know exactly what they want to do, while others keep taking every single test just to keep their parents off their backs. Here are a few tests and the reasons why GBAPs take them:

GRE— "I can avoid working for almost ten years if I decide to go for the Ph.D."

"I go to Spelman. I have to take one of those standardized tests in order to graduate."

"This test allows me to keep my options open."

GMAT—	"I can stomach working for a year or two before my next break."
	"I hated econ, but maybe I'll like business school more."
LSAT—	"Cool—I can hold off working for another three years."
	"Dad's paying—and I'll be able to do 'anything' with a law degree."
	"Well, I've already taken the GRE and the GMAT, and I know I'm not going to medical school."
MCAT—	"I'm definitely set on med school—my life's dream (not to mention my dad's) . . ."

Dating . . . It's No Longer PG

LET'S TALK ABOUT SEX

G: How to Trap a BAP

PG: The Kiss

PG-13:   The Art of Sharing a Twin Bed

R: The "Everything But" Club

NC-17:   Wild Thing

College dating is a once in a lifetime experience! For the first time, the BAP has no judgmental parents or nosy siblings hanging around to change the course of Cupid's arrows. Love blossoms everywhere like flowers in springtime—in the cafeteria, classrooms, at parties, the gym, even the library.

The pamphlet from the doctor's office, the insert from "the Pill" packet, and her mother's clinical discussions give the BAP a thumbnail sketch of sex. But ironically, these descriptions leave a lot to be desired. So in walks the sex guru, your dorm's Dr. Ruth. She's experienced and worldly. . . . Have questions? She can answer them. Don't know what the "wet spot" is? Not quite sure how to do something? This girl has been around the block a time or two. And, if you can put up with her smugness, you can learn all that you need to know (and then some) about sex *and* the opposite sex.

How to Trap a BAP

- A date off campus (to a nice restaurant) will go over extremely well—borrow someone's car.
- Study dates—why not get good grades and fall in love at the same time?
- Write her love letters, notes, and poems (be creative, use your imagination).
- Send her flowers—you'll win big points with her and her friends, too.
- Invite her to your fraternity or dormitory dance.
- Invite her out to dinner with you and your parents when they come to visit.
- Don't pressure her for sex; get to know one another.

Pucker Up

Kissing can express a bevy of emotions at the end of the date: a peck on the cheek means "Thanks, I had a good time"; a smack on the lips means "There may be more in store for you, big fella"; and if the BAP dares slip him some French action . . . she's definitely interested.

The Art of Sharing a Twin Bed

College dorm rooms usually come equipped with two twin-sized beds, which means that the planning and design of 12×12 rooms leaves out the dating factor. The art of sharing a twin bed is something that many college co-eds learn to perfect. In fact, spooning was invented on a college campus. (Well, doesn't that go without saying?) Just like spoons in a drawer are stacked snugly, so too are the bodies of college co-eds everywhere. The phenomenon of spooning carries over into life beyond the ivies. (Why else would two adults, in a king-sized bed, smush themselves together?) It's amazing, the more things change, the more they remain the same.

The "Everything But" Club
(aka, The Tease—but hey, there are worse names . . . like Easy)

A little hanky-panky never hurt anyone, right? Gauging whether it's your heart or your hormones propelling you forward is a delicate matter. Until you can read the Geiger counter clearly, we suggest waiting at least three months per beau for an accurate reading. For the BAP, changing one's status from virgin to vixen is a big step NOT to be taken lightly.

Wild Thing

Sexual intercourse, the horizontal mambo, the bedsheet tango . . . If you decide to take the plunge, make sure you're prepared. You would never take a shower without a shower cap, would you? Once the plunge is taken . . . for some there's no going back. Others employ the "don't touch *it*" school of discipline to get through those weak moments.

So You've Been to the Other Side

You made the plunge, but don't want to go there again and again and again. Here are a few things that'll keep you in check:
- Don't shave or wax your legs—you'll be too embarrassed to go too far.
- Don't bring mints—you'll be less likely to kiss him.
- Don't touch it.

The List

Don't pretend you don't know what it is . . . just try to keep your business to yourself. This college rating guide to the best lovers on campus sweeps the underground. Make sure that your name doesn't get on it. Being placed on *The List* would certainly qualify as conduct unbecoming a BAP.

BAP Quiz #3

Eric, the finest guy on campus, calls and asks a BAP to go to his fraternity ball. A few days later she finds out that he only asked her out to make the girl he really likes (the BAP's archenemy) jealous.

Match the response/action with the BAP:

a. Whatever, girl, he is *fine!* By the time the evening is over, he'll only have eyes for me.

b. I can't believe this guy . . . but I'm kind of flattered that he'd choose me to make that bubblehead jealous.

c. I've gotta call someone and get some advice on this one . . . it could make or break me.

d. I *knew* something strange was going on . . . glad I said I wasn't available. Who ever heard of going to a formal with someone you've never been on a date with?

a. Bogus   b. Boho   c. Butterfly   d. Betty.

Answer Key:

THE GOOD LIFE:
THE BAP ALL GROWN UP

Name: Betty Betty

Home: South Loop, Chicago, Illinois

Occupation: Attorney

Zodiac Sign: Virgo

Fondest Childhood Memory: Sailing on Sunday mornings with Dad, Sister, and the packed box lunches that Mom made

Favorite Restaurants: MKs and Grapes

Favorite Foods: Gnocchi, risotto, and sushi

Favorite Pig-Out Foods: French fries, olives, hummus, and pita chips

Favorite Vacation Spots:	St. Barth's and Maui
Hobbies:	Tennis, travel, golf, and photography
Favorite Designer:	Hard to choose . . . Prada, Ralph Lauren, Jil Sander . . . I love them all
Favorite Movie:	*The Best Man*
Ideal Man:	Does he exist?
Mom's Best Advice:	Don't move in with a man unless you're married to him . . . (Of course, it took a trial run for me to believe this. P.S. I'm still not married.)

Name:	Billie Boho
Home:	Venice Beach, Los Angeles, California
Occupation:	Curator, New World Exhibits, Getty Museum
Zodiac Sign:	Sagittarius
Fondest Childhood Memory:	Ice skating on our backyard pool
Favorite Restaurants:	Versailles and Ocean 7
Favorite Foods:	Crazy noodles with tofu, wraps, and Japanese curry
Favorite Pig-Out Foods:	Belgian *pommes frites*
Favorite Vacation Spots:	Jackson Hole; Maine; Portland, Oregon; and kayaking in Baja, Mexico
Hobbies:	Checking out new coffee shops and bookstores
Favorite Designer:	Whomever, whatever, whenever—the best are no names; but I do like Ana Sui; and a touch of Phat Farm
Favorite Movies:	*She's Gotta Have It* and *Rashomon*
Ideal Man:	Someone who will let me be me
Mom's Best Advice:	Always listen to your inner voice

Name:	Bonita Butterfly
Home:	Adams Morgan, Washington, D.C.
Occupation:	Physician
Zodiac Sign:	Leo
Fondest Childhood Memory:	Summers down South with Auntie Selma
Favorite Restaurants:	Houston's and Citron
Favorite Pig-Out Foods:	Salt n' Sour Potato Chips
Favorite Vacation Spots:	The Bahamas and down South
Hobbies:	Reading, antiquing, and bowling
Favorite Foods:	Chinese and sweet potato pie
Favorite Designer:	I'm a Banana Republic girl, but I'm learning to love Cynthia Rowley, Max Mara, and Ralph (oh no, I'm turning into a Betty).
Favorite Movie:	*The Wood*
Ideal Man:	Just a nice guy with a good head on his shoulders
Mom's Best Advice:	Keep your nose to the grindstone. Believe in yourself and you can do anything.

Name:	Barbara Bogus
Home:	Buckhead, Atlanta, Georgia
Occupation:	Homemaker
Zodiac Sign:	Gemini
Fondest Childhood Memory:	Being invited to Jack and Jill parties
Favorite Restaurants:	Justin's (owned by no other than Sean "Puffy" Combs) and The Food Studio
Favorite Foods:	Caviar and lobster thermidor
Favorite Pig-Out Foods:	Flamin' Hot Cheetos
Favorite Vacation Spot:	Las Vegas
Hobbies:	Vegas, Vegas, Vegas
Favorite Movie:	*Booty Call*
Favorite Designer:	I prefer Versace, I love Donatella's colorful touch!
Ideal Man:	Anyone breathing who has a phat bank account
Mom's Best Advice:	Fake it 'til you make it.

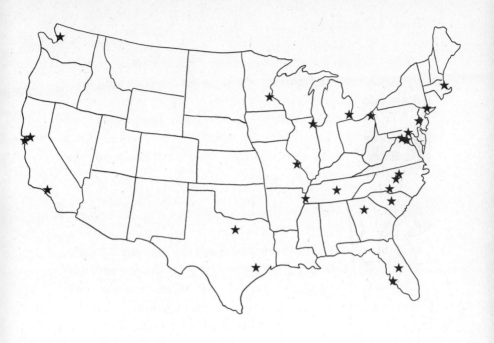

Where the BAPs Are

Alexandria, Va. ★ Arlington, Va. ★ Atlanta ★ Austin, Tex. ★
Baltimore, Md. ★ Boston ★ Charlotte, N.C. ★ Chicago ★
Columbia, S.C. ★ Dallas ★ Denver ★ Detroit ★ Houston ★
Kansas City, Mo. ★ Los Angeles ★ Memphis ★ Miami ★
Minneapolis ★ Nashville ★ New Orleans ★ New York ★
Oakland ★ Orlando ★ Philadelphia ★ Phoenix ★ Pittsburgh
★ Raleigh-Durham, N.C. ★ San Francisco ★ Sarasota ★
Seattle ★ Shaker Heights, Ohio ★ Silver Spring, Md. ★ St. Louis
★ Washington, D.C.

BAP Lifestyles

The Big City holds a veritable cornucopia of fun and frolicking for the BAP. Undeterred by exorbitant rents, she figures "Why not? If the money didn't go toward rent or a mortgage, I'd spend it at Barney's anyway!!!" Generally, BAPs prefer buildings with doormen and alarm systems that are located in "safe" neighborhoods. But leave it to a Boho to move into the diciest area in a city and call herself a pioneer for the new millennium.

Boomerang BAPs

An Australian BAP? Not quite. This moniker aptly applies to BAPs who, no matter how far away they go—Europe, California, even South Africa—they *always* return home (aka the BAParents' worst dream come true). Her motto is *"Su casa es mi casa"* forever.

Maternal Admonitions for Boomerang BAPs

1. Clean up your room.
2. If you would just hang up your clothes after you take them off . . .
3. You don't have enough for a down payment? Don't worry, we'll help you. Just get out!
4. You're spending the night where? With whom? You'd better hope your key still works in the morning!
5. I hope you're not planning to wear *that* on your date!
6. Look, I'll buy you a coat if you promise not to wear that old raggedy one.
7. Who made these calls to New Zealand?
8. I don't care how old you are, you call when you're out late.
9. You sure are spending a lot of money going to see that boy.
10. What are you doing with your life?
11. If you are going to drive my car, it doesn't run on empty. . . . Put gas in it.
12. You're an adult now—you'd better get it together!
13. It's time for you to move on.
14. Go move in with that boy and see how quickly your love lasts.
15. Make sure you clean up—the housekeeper's coming tomorrow.

Workin' 9 to 5 (and beyond) . . .

At some point, unless she gets married early to someone rich and famous, the BAP's stint as a professional student comes to a grinding halt (how many degrees does one legitimately need?). For some BAPs the segue from freedom to responsibility is a breeze; for others, entering the frantic work world is about as enjoyable as doing the polar bear swim in Lake Michigan on an early December morning. Secretly, many BAPs are striving to become their own bosses or, as quiet as it's kept, the consummate housewife. . . . But until that time . . . they toil and burn the midnight oil.

You Know a BAP Is Stressed Out at Work If:

1. She bursts into tears (for any reason).
2. She takes a personal sanity day and goes insane anyway because her office calls her at home with dumb questions all day.
3. She needs a therapist to deal with her job.
4. Her therapist prescribes Prozac.
5. She's beyond evil when she answers the phone.

To: MrsBetty@housewife.com
From: bettybetty@largelawfirm.com

Mom—
I'm really sorry I've been so unavailable. I really do want to hear about Alan and Cynthia's new house, but I've been totally swamped. Would you believe, I have been working 12–14 hour days for the past three weeks? I am exhausted. If I don't fall asleep, I'll call you from the car on my way home.
Betty

From: MrsBetty@housewife.com
To: bettybetty@largelawfirm.com

Dear, I'm sorry to hear about your work schedule. Does this mean that the dark circles under your eyes are worse?
Love, Mother

Why the BAP Needs a Wife

Bigamy is not a problem if an additional wife will help get your life organized!

Q: What happened to the BAP who ran out of clean underwear?

A: On her way to work, she stopped at Bloomies and bought ten new pairs.

Mmmm, dinner is piping hot, made just the way the BAP likes it. Her clothes are carefully hung and folded, with her suits arranged by fabric and designer as she requested. All of the BAP's worries melt away in the hot bath drawn for her, scented candles circling the tub. Who is this miracle worker in her midst? It certainly isn't the BAP. It's her wife.

In her dreams! Hey, men have known this for eons—in order to maintain their sanity, they realize that a wife is the ticket! Can you cook dinner, clean the condo, pick up the dry cleaning, do the dishes, pay the bills, pick out that special birthday gift, bring home the bacon, take care of the kids, and look FAB-U-LOUS all at the same time? Girl, stop kidding yourself . . . *dream on!*

In the BAP's World, a Wife Would:

1. Pay her bills on time.
2. Balance her checkbook.
3. Give her a weekly allowance.
4. Clean her house/apartment or hire a cleaning lady.
5. Take her clothes to the dry cleaners and pick them up.
6. Take her shoes to be repaired.
7. Go to the grocery store and buy food for well-balanced meals (cheese and crackers, PB&J sandwiches, and cottage cheese do not count as balanced meals!).
8. Organize her social calendar and return phone calls.

9. Have the car serviced.
10. Just make her life easier!

Why the BAP Is Never Too Young to Hire a Housekeeper

- She has too many other more important things to do than clean.
- She doesn't want to ruin her weekly manicure.
- She didn't clean as a child, so why start now?
- She has one more thing to schedule her hair appointment around.
- Her time can be better spent relaxing.
- She wouldn't want to ruin her hands with all of those harsh chemicals.
- It's better to hire someone to do the dirty work.

Maternal Admonitions for BAPs All Grown Up

1. Work is not a four-letter word.
2. I paid for four years of college, and two years of grad school, and you want to join the Peace Corps?
3. How do you have money to go to the Ski Summit, but you don't have money to pay your parking tickets?
4. How many Prada moments can one girl have?
5. You need to start dressing like an adult now.
6. When is your next hair appointment?
7. Don't work so hard that you forget to get married.
8. You're always at work—when do you find the time to date?
9. You just need to go ahead and hire a housekeeper.
10. What do you mean you're going to live in a walk-up? Don't you need a doorman?

Instant Message
From: anoldersister@standinghairappt.com
To: littlesister@badblowdry.com
Subject: hi

So how did your hair turn out? I can't believe you tried to do it yourself!

From: littlesister@badblowdry.com
To: anoldersister@standinghairappt.com
Subject: hi

Oh my God, it was awful!!! I started roundbrushing the back of my head and did one section in the back. Then I went up about an inch and started doing the next section. Well, either my brush was too small or my hair was too long, and the combination of those two factors created a disaster. My hair rolled around the brush more than once and got stuck (I don't know how). It took me about 15 minutes to get my hair untangled. At one point I seriously contemplated cutting it because I was so panic-stricken. After I detangled my hair, I decided to skip the round brush technique and I just blew it the regular way. But my hair nightmare doesn't end there. As you know, my curling iron is broken, a fact I had forgotten until it was time to curl my hair. So I had two choices: a flat iron or large barrel curling iron that goes from hot to boiling in 60 seconds. I chose the flat iron. All I can say is that it looks full.

Down to the Roots: BAP Hair

It is the bane of her existence. It is her crown and glory. It is . . . BAP hair. Consumed with thoughts about her hair from the moment she turns on the morning news, pressing world issues are shoved aside so that the BAP can attack her hair! Whether her hair is relaxed, braided, locked, or natural, BAPs are on a constant quest for the perfect hairstyle. Just how difficult is this? Some compare it to climbing Mount Everest barefoot. Ideally, a BAP wants to wake, shake, and go, but realistically that ain't gonna happen. First, a BAP has to find a hairstylist she likes; then she has to find the perfect hairstyle. Hair should be the first thing that people notice about a BAP because it's healthy; not because she looks like a Patti LaBelle impersonator on crack, or because her hair stands twenty feet off her head or looks like a scaled-down amusement park ride.

Afro, Afro, Go Away—The Frizz Factor

Moisture is the BAP's arch-nemesis. Her hair is capable of going "kizzy" at just the hint of rain. It's a well-kept secret that the Weather Channel uses BAP hair to gauge humidity. The threat of an increased dew point keeps the BAP on her toes. That's why she's never without her handy-dandy emergency humidity kit: a soft-bristled brush to smooth the edges, a headband, a hair clip, a ponytail holder, gel, and, in case of dire emergency, a baseball cap.

Fit or Fly?

Exercise simply has to be scheduled around hair appointments. Who could fathom a weekend workout with a hot date planned? The only BAP who's perfected the art of being fit and fly simultaneously is Oprah. Relaxed and thermal styles require planning and a portable salon. Blow-dryers, curling irons, sheens, sprays, pomades, and conditioners all help to keep the frizzies at bay. If the BAP gets her hair done on Friday, she won't go back to the gym until Monday so she can look good all weekend, of course.

If You Can't Achieve It, Weave It!

"What do you mean it's a weave?" "That's not your hair?" "Well, I guess it's yours, you paid for it." Contrary to popular belief, a weave is acceptable as long as it doesn't look like one (that is, the tracks

aren't showing, and it doesn't look like a toupee, or a "threepee" for that matter). A weave is nothing to be embarrassed by as long as it's well maintained. It is a lifestyle choice.

All Locked Up

Braids, locks, twists, and naturals best epitomize low-maintenance hairstyles and afford the BAP peace of mind and a helluva lot more time! The time it takes to get braids or to grow locks is well worth it. This BAP, once a slave to her hair, is now liberated from the passion of the hot comb. No longer controversial, a plethora of textured styles can now be found everywhere from the operating room to the board-room.

BAP Quiz #4

The BAP's regular hairstylist, someone she has been going to for years, decides to relocate out of town.

Match each BAP's reaction to the responses below.

1. She's sorry to see her go, but quickly gets over it and calls a few friends for recommendations.
2. At first she's devastated and feels as if it is a national crisis. But ever-resourceful, she pools her funds with several other distressed clients and flies the hairstylist back to town every two weeks.
3. So what, she can always find a better stylist with a more impressive clientele.
4. It's not a big deal. She was thinking about locking her hair anyway.

Answer Key:
1. Butterfly   2. Betty   3. Bogus   4. Boho.

BAP Hair on the Go

BAPs no longer have to fear being caught in a city with no idea of where to go to get their hair done. Here is a list of some BAP favorites.

ATLANTA
Charles Gregory Hair Salon, 2870 Peachtree Road, Suite 458, Atlanta, GA 30305 (770) 622–0696.
The Purple Door, 836 Beecher St. SW, Atlanta, GA 30310 (404) 755–2996.

BOSTON

Olive's Beauty Salon, 565 Columbus Ave., Boston, MA 02118 (617) 247–3333.

CHICAGO

Nuzhet Sayran at Pascal Pour Elle, 507 N. Wells, Chicago, IL 60610 (312) 670–7007.

Toss Hair Salon, 1020 S. Wabash, Chicago, IL 60605 (312) 986–8677.

Van Cleef Hair Studio, 56 W. Huron, Chicago, IL 60610 (312) 751–2456.

Visionaries, 357 W. Chicago Ave., Chicago, IL 60610 (312) 337–4700.

DETROIT

Mane Taming, 19883 Livernois, Detroit, MI 48221 (313) 255–8650.

Meagan Mitchell Salon, 1376 Broadway, Detroit, MI 48226 (313) 967–0650.

Evelynn McConney, Precision Hair Design, 1062 W. Huron, Waterford, MI 48238 (248) 681–7633.

Mel's Beauty Salon, 6080 Woodward Ave., Detroit, MI 48202 (313) 872–6630.

LOS ANGELES

Oh My Nappy Hair, 805 S. LaBrea Ave., Los Angeles, CA 90036 (323) 939–3992.

John Atchison, 8232 W. 3rd St., Los Angeles, CA 90048 (323) 655–2887.

NEW YORK

Marcy's Images, Hair, Nail and Facial Salon, 54 W. 31st Street, 3rd Floor, New York, NY 10001 (212) 889–9540/52.

Dawn Joi at The Joi, call (312) 943–9797 in Chicago (by appointment only in New York and Chicago).

Hair Styling by Joseph, Inc., 113 E. 60th Street, New York, NY 10022 (212) 355–6965.

Instant Message
From: bbutterfly@columbiamed.edu.
To: childhoodfriend@goldman.com
Subject: hi

I don't know what I'm turning into. I had to take my photo for the
face book today and it's about week 7 . . . my naps are just all over
the place, plus I worked out last night . . . so I had to go get my "do"
did before I could come to work. Of course Marcy doesn't open until
10am and was closed yesterday, so today she was booked (I just
showed up thinkin' it would be empty on Wednesday A.M. and when I
said I had to be at work by 12:30 the other clients looked at me and I
know they were thinking: Is she for real or what?) . . . Got to the
hospital and everyone said, "Oh my God, your hair looks great!" (I
wanted to say, "Well, damn, do I usually just look bad or what?")
Anyway, one Black nurse just screamed out, "Girl, your hair is amazing, did you get it done this morning?" So much for my secret.

There are distinct differences between BAP and BAMA hairstyles:

BAPs weave, BAMAs weev.
BAPs have hair-DOs, BAMAs have hair-DON'Ts.
BAPs highlight their hair, BAMAs' hair products double as art supplies.
The BAP's motto is, "If you can't achieve it, weave it!"
The BAMA's motto is, "If it looks real, it's not long enough."

Wig Whipping Tips—The BAP's Short List to Finding the Right Stylist

Make sure she or he:

1. Has their own hair—or the receipt for it.
2. Believes cleanliness is next to godliness.
3. Knows how to tell time.
4. Doesn't book clients like an air traffic controller at O'Hare.
5. Believes that fingernails aren't an avenue of artistic expression.

Who Says Beauty is Only Skin-Deep?

The BAP Beauty Regimen

- Weekly hair appointment
- Weekly manicure
- Monthly pedicure
- Monthly facial
- Monthly massage
- Monthly brow, bikini, and underarm waxing
- Facial peel every three months

Favorite BAP Spas

1. New York—Bliss
2. Chicago—Kiva
3. Los Angeles—Beverly Hills Hot Springs
4. Atlanta—Key Lime Pie
5. Washington, DC—Andre Chreky
6. Santa Fe, NM—Ten Thousand Waves
7. Dallas, TX—The Greehouse Spa

If Clothes Make the Woman, Accessories Make the BAP

The average BAP is not a trust fund baby, so she may not have an all-designer closet. But you will find that she has the authentic accessories that count . . . an Hermès scarf, a Gucci belt . . . read on for the must-haves.

Chic Shades

The object is to look cool but not too cool; to have that familiar look, that "I may be a star" look. Really, glasses should complement, not overpower. Oliver Peoples, Mikli's, Gucci, and others will do the trick!

A Few Fun Hats

 For those bad hair days or just to look cute. From baseball caps to funky hats, there's no better way to top off a BAP!

Earrings

 Start with the basics and build from there. Pearl and diamond studs will do to start. By the way, it is okay to go fake, but just don't overdo it on the cubic zirconium carats, please!

| Scarves | An Hermès scarf is the must-have of all must-haves. A pocket or full square—it doesn't matter. They're all beautiful. If nothing else, it's a great conversation piece. |  |

Jewelry — At least one or two Tiffany pieces . . . maybe a fun bracelet or choker. (Yes, sterling is fine!) Just a little something to tide you over until bigger and better things come your way. A watch? *Oui*, or *non*? Heirlooms work well as do Rolex, Cartier, Patek Phillipe, or even Timex. 'Tis a personal thing—style it, baby!

Belts — A classic croc belt or croc knockoff. Plain jane leather in black and brown, and a funky/trendy one à la Gucci or Prada.

Makeup — No BAP can live without a great foundation, a few terrific lipsticks, and mascara for that put-together, *au naturel* look. Try Liz Arden's Skin Matching System—it's to die for. MAC's always got the perfect lipstick and mascara.

Staples

Classic Blazers	Calvin, Jil Sander, or even Banana Republic—all's well that hangs well! To be worn with an accompanying skirt or slacks, or casual slim pants or jeans.
Leather or Suede	Need we say more? The ultimate luxe item to dress up or down.
Jeans	Comfy, plain, or decorated, everybody's got a pair of jeans they just love. To slum in on the weekend or for a night out on the town, jeans are always in.
Cotton Shirts	Great for work or play—easy to dress up or down, the cotton shirt just works all around. A fresh look in white, blue, or any other color you'd like to do! (Launder me with starch, please.)
Twin Sets	Once a staple of the '50s, now a staple of the millennium and beyond. Great to have in a rainbow of colors to create that feminine look!

Shoes, Glorious Shoes

High heels and flats. Patent leather and *peau de soie.* Boots and sandals. BAPs love them all! There's nothing worse than having the perfect outfit and imperfect shoes—it can ruin one's whole day (so much so that at lunch a BAP may have to run out and buy a new pair). A BAP can never have too many pairs of shoes (Imelda would be proud).

Athletic/Funky

Big soles, funky treads, or odd-shaped toe boxes, BAPs draw their inspiration from the hottest trends on the streets—granted, the street is smack-dab in the middle of SoHo, but BAP footwear is sometimes about being on the cutting edge. For the more athletically inclined, there are shoes for every sport: golf cleats, running shoes, aerobic, and cross trainers. The key is functionality with a flair. Nike, New Balance, and Adidas are some favorites.

Loafers

Gucci, the granddaddy of the designer loafer, has inspired many a high-profile progeny, but Prada is clearly the genius of the family, turning the staid look on its head by adding a little funk to the familiar. Whether in fabric or leather, standard sole or chunky funky, the loafer captures both the conservative and *joie de vivre* of BAPdom.

Mules

The aptly named workhorse of the shoe family, mules can take a chic chick from work to play and back again (but preferably not back). Some of the BAPs' fave designers are TOD's, Ralph, Cynthia Rowley, Cole Haan, and Manolo Blahnik for that va-va-va-voom appeal.

Pumps

Manolo Blahniks and Jimmy Choo are two of the finest purveyors of modern couture footwear. These shoes come adorned with handblown glass beads, exotic fabrics, and backbreaking heels. These pumps are eclectic and sexy. A must-have for anyone over thirty.

Standard pumps for everyday wear like Ferragamo, Via Spiga, or Gucci are the BAPs' choice for presenting that non-froufrou image to the corporate world. (There's plenty of time for that later.)

Strappy Sandals

When you simply *have* to show off that special pedicure, what better way than with a pair of bejeweled Kate Spades, Charles Davids, or

Sigerson Morrison. Recent popular styles are Chinese-style thongs, pony hair, and strappy high-heeled leather sandals. It's all about smooth legs and pretty toes—get the hint?

Wedge

A simple slip-on that gives you height without giving you bunions and bad ankles, the wedge is another staple of the shoe closet. Robert Clergerie stands heel and sole above the rest. Espace, Clergerie's funky offshoot, is equally appealing and a bit lighter on the wallet. Donald J. Pliner makes a mean little athletic and wavy-soled shoe for the funky-fresh BAP.

Ubiquitous Perennials

Some solid standbys that every BAP must have (please choose from among the following brands): Barney's private label, which always has terrific knockoffs, Cole Haan, David Aaron, Kenneth Cole, Birkenstocks, and Enzo. All of the above shoes won't crunch your feet or your wallet.

Some BAP Advice

The Importance of Having Plenty of Black Shoes

Having a plethora of black shoes is like having a stable full of prize-winning racehorses—they'll never let you down. Sure, you will probably have to stand in front of the mirror wearing at least three different pairs before you can decide on the right shoes for that particular day, but the alternative (having to settle for a pair of shoes because that's all you've got) just isn't palatable!

The Quest for Perfection

The quest for perfection when buying shoes often leads one astray . . . the shoes might feel good for a few steps in the store and look great on your feet, *but* you just hadn't anticipated walking ten city blocks in those bad boys! Now, they gotta go.

Manolo Beware, the BAPs are on a Shopping Spree!

Pay five hundred dollars or more for a pair of shoes? You gotta be kidding, right? Well, the joke's on you. . . . A five-hundred-dollar pair of shoes may severely cut into your shoe budget, but, girl, your dogs will have no need to bark!

It's All in the Bag

What BAP would be caught rompin' around town without the perfect handbag? There are just too many to choose from—oversized to tiny. (BAP Note: nondistinguishable fakes are fine . . . if you must)—read on for a few favorites.

Kate Spade	The basic bag with a little twist. But, always with KS style!
Gucci	An oldie but a goodie! Talk about staying power, today's styles are not quite as "logo-ed," but very sleek and to die for.
Prada	Miuccia brought parachute material to the scene! Every BAP has at least one Prada item whether it's a wallet, a makeup bag, or a purse. She's gotta have it!
Louis Vuitton	Good ole LV has come back to town with classics and then some. LV has brought great color to a bag that will last forever. The classic LV bag is still

	hot! And the new leathers? They're absolutely fabulous!
Coach	The old standard still stands and the new designs are amazing. Good quality, all-American bags for the all-American BAP. They do stand the test of time. Betty still has one from fifth grade.
Cynthia Rowley	The best little evening bags in the country for the minimalist in you. And, we're talking really little!
Fendi	*Fendissimo.* The chic little bag of the millennium.
Chanel	What more can we say?
Hermès	The Kelly bag will *always* be in.
Burberry	A little change of name never hurt anyone! Gotta love that signature plaid.
TOD's	The Italian who wants to be English. Sorry, you can't fake the funk with these beautiful bags.

You Wear It Well—Ten Great Coats

RuPaul, diva extraordinaire, wouldn't be caught dead without her "do" in place, MAC on her face, an outfit skintight, and her coat just right. Whether you live in Alaska or Zaire—the perfect wrap is essential. Mom has a closetful and you should, too.

1. Long Trench—Basic Burberry.
2. Short Trench/Duster—Barbour, *bébé.*
3. Wool Car Coat—Max Mara won't let you down.
4. Shearling Darling—Nothing else will keep you warmer—an acceptable fur for the nonfur gal!
5. Full-Fledged Swing—It don't mean a thing, if you ain't got that swing!
6. A Mommy Fur—There's certainly nothing wrong with a hand-me-down.

7. Your Own Fur—You go, Girl!
8. Down Jacket—Gotta be able to keep warm on the slopes.
9. Leather Jacket—Just looks cool.
10. A Krazy Koat—An abfab fun funky coat that you love—a fun fur, pony hair, leopard or zebra print, girls just wanna have fun!

Instant Message
From: scole@compulsiveshoppingdisorder.com
To: bettyb@shopaholic.com
Subject: hi

How was your Hermès weekend? By the way, I'm going to the doctor. I think I'm suffering from compulsive shopping disorder. I like to call it CSD.

From: bettyb@shopaholic.com
To: scole@compulsiveshoppingdisorder.com
Subject: hi

My Hermès weekend was great, can you believe I got a scarf on sale? It was topped off by my first purchase of Prada shoes (at the outlet mall). I think I've just outdone myself (they were $90) in a matter of a few days. I'm reveling in my new purchases. I told my mother I needed a wife to take care of my finances for me. She said she'd get all of my bills in the computer and pay them directly. I said thank God!

Veni, Vidi, Vendi . . .

. . . I Came, I Saw, I Shopped

Life's little ills are sometimes best cured by a

good dose of shopping. Yet, nary a cure has been found for Compulsive Shopping Disorder (CSD), a disease

that runs in the BAP bloodline. Remember the BAPgirl Incentive Program? It was simply the precursor to CSD. This disease involves treating yourself to something you deserve, and you always deserve something! (The disease is contagious—Butterflies and Boguses

have been known to become severely afflicted.)

CSD is liable to take over one's mind, body, and soul at any time

(due to great happiness or sorrow, a raise, a new job, a new boyfriend, a breakup, a vacation, you name it). Then, without warning, usually when the credit card bills start rolling in or the savings account begins to sag a little too much, it goes into remission for a week, a month, or even a year (okay, so a year is rare). Fortunately, at least in the BAP's eyes (but not her bank account's), a cure has yet to be discovered.

Where BAPs Love to Shop

- Barney's of New York (BAPs of North America)
- Saks Fifth Avenue (she never abandons her training ground)
- Banana Republic (don't underestimate the power of the GAP)
- Anthropologie (when she needs funky threads in a flash)
- Henri Bendel's (the best accessories for her coifro)
- Bloomingdales (to fill up her big BAP shopping bag)
- Neiman Marcus (a BAP staple)
- Cynthia Rowley (need a dress in a hurry? Cynthia won't fail her)
- Kenneth Cole (purses, shoes, and coats—what more can a girl ask for?)
- Local unique boutiques (doesn't want to run the risk of looking like someone else)
- Nordstrom (shoes galore)

Top BAP Outlets

1. New York—Woodbury Commons
2. Los Angeles—Desert Hills Premium Outlet, The Citadel, Barstow Tanger Factory Outlets
3. Chicago—The Lighthouse and Kenosha Outlets
4. San Francisco—Napa Premium Outlets
5. Atlanta—North Georgia Premium Outlets
6. Miami—Sawgrass Mills
7. Boston—Wrentham Village Premium Outlets; Manchester Outlets (Vermont)
8. Philadelphia—Franklin Mills Mall
9. Detroit—Great Lakes Crossing

A BAP Daydream

Curing CSD—A BAP Shopaholic Goes to Betty Ford

Only Betty Ford's intensive rehab program could cure a shopaholic BAP.

Picture it—the BAP and her counselor at Saks:

Betty Ford counselor: Put the Prada down! Back away from the counter, slowly.

BAP: But this would look so great with my Gucci loafers. (She goes for her wallet.)

Betty Ford counselor: Don't touch that credit card!

The BAP hands it to the salesperson with total abandon.

Betty Ford counselor: One more purchase?!?! she asks, with a total look of terror on her face.

The dulcet tones of the BAP's credit information traveling across phone lines and satellites fills the air.

BAP: Oh, it will be all right, I have plenty of room.

Tick, tick, tick as she waits for approval from the great Credit God.

Betty Ford counselor: *Run!* It's gonna blow!!!

Miraculously it goes through. Yet another satisfying BAP moment.

The Butterfly Tae Kwon Do School of Shopping

White belt:	Goes shopping only when she *needs* something
Yellow belt:	Goes shopping when she *wants* something
Green belt:	Understands that shopping is a sport
Blue belt:	Learns the importance of quality over quantity
Red belt:	Discovers that a dollar saved is an accessory lost

| Brown belt: | Accessories. Accessories. Accessories. She can't buy enough |
| Black belt: | CSD sets in |

Love Jones—BAPs on Romance

Some say the BAP's standards are too high. Is it too much to ask for a guy who's intelligent, cute, ambitious, witty, outgoing, fun . . . you know, an equal, someone perfect just like her?

The Dating Game

Dating, while technically an individual sport, is a team sport for BAPs. It requires an agent, coach, a referee, and general manager. One individual may embody all these positions or these roles may be farmed out to a multitude of friends and/or family members.

Agent (aka, Busybody)

This friend does the legwork, researches and suggests eligible bachelors, reviews the latest restaurants and clubs for future dates, and will occasionally get on the BAP's last nerve. The agent is a vital member of the team because without her dogged pursuit of "Mr. Right" instead of "Mr. Right Now," she spares her friend the agony of dating "The Sweetest Taboo" (see below).

Coach (aka, been there—done that)

This is the friend who has seen it all, knows all the moves, and has a playbook that rivals John Thompson's. She has twelve responses to the "failure to call after the date" play and is willing to do your hair in an emergency. Yeah, she's single, but with her knowledge one of you is bound to end up in a long-term relationship!

Referee (aka, call me if you need me)

This is usually one of his friends, male or female. The ref acts as an interpreter for both sides. Until the team (i.e., couple) is a cohesive unit, each player often runs into strategy problems because they don't understand the signals being given by the other. The ref interprets his plays for her and, if asked, analyzes her playbook with him.

General Manager (aka, the Dating Dalai Lama)

General manager is the prestigious position usually conferred on a married friend or a mother/maternal figure. She doesn't have time to deal with the daily crises. She sees the big picture—getting you married. She'll suggest ways for you to maintain your relationship, explain the virtues of the big c word (compromise), and guide you through the obstacle course leading up to marriage. She poses the hard questions: "Do you love him?" "Can you live with him forever?" If the response is "No," she'll tell you to move on. If the response is "I'm not sure," she'll tell you to move on. Any hesitation will be met with "He's not the one— you'll know him when you meet him."

The Sweetest Taboo

He didn't go to college? He's white? He's a mechanic? He's your dad's age? These are the questions BAPs who date men outside of their tight-knit social circle encounter from friends and family members. Some would say that these women are wayward BAPs who must be brought back into the fold. Others postulate that these young ladies are looking for true love regardless of the package. Is the age-old saying that "opposites attract" true in the world of BAP dating? Well, some like to think so. A BAP who dates a man who is significantly older or younger, or one who is culturally, racially, or socioeconomically diverse from her, may be in for a roller-coaster ride. But if her daily life starts to resemble the "Demon Drop" instead of "It's a Small World," she can always go back to the magical world of BAPdom.

Check 'Em Out—A BAP Pre-Date Checklist

1. Check out his shoes and clothes. Are they totally synthetic? If so, just imagine the gifts he'll buy you.
2. Clean fingernails? Are they longer than yours?
3. Is he a sloppy dresser? Still has marinara stains from last week's lunch? Drop that zero and get a hero!
4. Good strong teeth and gums—hey, if he can't take care of his teeth, what will he do with a family?

So You're Interested . . . A Game Plan for Staying Cool

1. Don't give out your home number. Take his and call him if you still have the feeling.
2. Chat by phone or e-mail first—is he witty? Can he make you laugh?
3. Call your agent. See if she knows him, or if she knows someone else who knows him.

You Can Tell You're Dating a BAP When. . . .

1. She spends ten minutes talking to the waiter before she orders.
2. Imelda Marcos calls her to borrow shoes.

3. You can only go to the gym together on her off-hair day.
4. There's no room in her closet to hang your suits.
5. She's not the best domestic engineer.
6. She's always right (guys, it's easier to just let her be).

First Date Tips . . . For Him

1. Be on time . . . but don't expect her to be (yes, it's a double standard—get used to it).
2. Defer to her, she's the captain of the *Love Boat.*
3. Suppress your urge to wear polyester or your father's dashiki.
4. A man who talks about his ex-girlfriend is on his way to creating the next one.
5. Be up front about previous or impending offspring.
6. Leave "Tyrone" at home.
7. Chivalry is not dead—it's only on life support—revive it.

You Know She's Smitten When She. . . .

1. Introduces you to her parents.
2. Cooks for you.
3. Asks your advice on important matters.
4. Takes time out to talk to you when you call her at work.
5. Cleans up after you.
6. Nurses you when you're sick.
7. Does nice things for you.

Drop That Zero—Telltale Signs He's Not the One. . . .

1. He can't speak the King's English.
2. He does not believe in stay-at-home moms.
3. He never invites you to his house.
4. He believes that his mom should stay at home—that's why he still lives with her.
5. His fingernails are longer than yours.
6. His hair puts Al Sharpton's and James Brown's to shame.
7. He has a gold tooth and/or a curl.
8. He wears enough gold for a Mr. T starter kit.
9. Stacy Adams are his shoes and not an ex-girlfriend.
10. His suits are identical to the colors of a Now and Later variety pack.
11. You only have his pager number—for Domino's Pizza.

A Bridge Over Troubled Water

A shoulder to cry on. The perfect escort. Handsome. Just like the brother you never had . . . great friend. Everyone thinks he's a great guy—you do, too. He's even attractive. At one point you would've considered dating him if only you hadn't been so into what's-his-name when you first met. Can you say, missed the boat?

At some point in her life, every BAP has a male friend who plays an integral role in her life—tells her she's wonderful when what's-his-name seems to have misplaced her phone number . . . fills in as her date at those god-awful work functions . . . eases the angst between what's-his-name and Prince Charming . . . a bridge on the path to adulthood. Fortunately, some of us have been smart enough to realize that the guy who takes the time to remember the names of all the what's-his-names might be a keeper. For the not-so-fortunate? Well, maybe they'll wake up before it's too late!

Instant Message
From: abetty@beggarscantbechoosers.com
To: anotherbetty@nolaymen.com
Subject: Would You Date a UPS Guy?

. . . . you crack me up!! I would date the UPS guy if he were fine, spoke in complete sentences, had a good personality, and had some kind of drive. Maybe a business of his own he's trying to get together, or if he has aspirations of climbing the corporate ladder at UPS. (By the way, is he the delivery guy?) . . . funny how time and not having a man can make you reconsider.

Still a Friend of Mine

The BAP has spent a lifetime cultivating her friends from the finest gardens in BAPdom. A little stress at work, a new boyfriend, a husband, or a distant locale will not prevent her from maintaining those friendships.

Frequent Flyers

Traveling for major events—graduate school graduations, major birthday celebrations, bridal showers, weddings, baby showers, spa weekends, and the like, or simply just because—are some ways BAPs cultivate their friendships.

Going Away? . . . The Bare Essentials

- √ PJs—white eyelet nightgown
- √ Underwear (always pack an extra pair just in case)
- √ Putty silk pants
- √ Blue cotton shirt
- √ Cashmere sweater

√ Pearl earrings and necklace
√ Prada loafers
√ Black pants
√ Gray pants
√ White shirt
√ Socks
√ Sleeveless black shell
√ Black Hermès scarf
√ Gucci belt
√ Black v-neck sweater or blue v-neck sweater or both
√ Black funky heels
√ Extra sweater
√ Burgundy DK sweater
√ MAC Diva lipstick
√ Brown mascara—Body Shop
√ Field's—free Elizabeth Arden sample
√ Lipliner—chestnut—MAC
√ Levi's

Pack in LV duffel

Drinks, Anyone?

Cosmopolitans, vodka tonics, Margaritas, and the like taste so much better when sipped in the company of good friends at the latest hotspot. Meeting for drinks after work or on the weekend makes way for great advice sessions, gossips, people-watching, or flirting with the guys across the bar.

The BAP smart set drinks nothing but Martinis. Its rumored that the Martini was created in New York at the Knickerbocker Hotel by an Italian immigrant named Martini di Arma di Taggia in the early 1900s. Not concerned with who created it, BAPs are helping to ensure that the iconoclastic stature of the Martini glass is here to stay—who doesn't look sexy holding one? A BAP's ability to hold her liquor will determine whether she prefers the real thing—vodka or gin—or one of its sweeter bastardized versions.

The Art of Martini Making

It's an absolute must to have a well-stocked bar; alcohol as well as stemware. Your bar should include a stainless-steel shaker, at least eight Martini glasses, a pitcher with a stirrer (for those who prefer theirs the opposite of 007, i.e., not shaken), gin and/or vodka, garnish skewers, olives, and plenty of ice. Whether serving them straight-up or on the rocks, gin or vodka, it takes just the right touch to make the perfect Martini.

Vodka
6 parts vodka (we prefer
Belvedere or Ketel One)
2 parts dry vermouth
Olives

Gin
6 parts gin (Tanqueray
Silver or Bombay Sapphire)
2 parts dry vermouth
$1/2$ tsp sweet vermouth
Lemon twist

Combine liquid ingredients in a cocktail shaker filled with cracked ice, and shake well. Strain into chilled Martini glass and garnish appropriately. For the lightweights, variations have been created to appease their less sophisticated palates, the most popular being the Cosmopolitan. The following list of some of the other more popular Sweetinis has forced bartenders across the country to step up to the plate:

Apple Martini
Chocolate Martini

Campari Martini

Crantini

Dirty Martini

Gibson

Gimlet

Lemon Drop

Manhattan

The Metropolitan

Negroni

Rum Martini (we prefer Bacardi)

Saketini

Tequini

Instant Message
From: bogus@will&graceweekend.com
To: singlefriend@onlythelonely.com
Subject: Fag Hag Weekend

Okay, I had a *Will and Grace* weekend, Jim was in town. Wednesday
night we went to dinner with his best friend here (Eric) it was hilarious . . . Thursday night we had a dinner party at a restaurant—8 gay
men (all very attractive with good jobs), me and Jennifer. Jennifer
was completely overwhelmed (Portia now calls me a fag hag). Friday
night we met at a restaurant in Times Square because Eric's good
friend is in a Broadway musical and the restaurant was across the
street from the rehearsal. Saturday, Jim and I went to the outlet mall
(Gucci and Prada, it was amazing)—we sat down once we got our map
and highlighted the stores we wanted to go to, then colored them in
on the map and then charted our course. Saturday night Eric and his
boyfriend had us over for dinner—we listened to show tunes (I kid you
not!!). By Sunday I was worn out!

Shopping, Lunching, and Brunching

All three provide for great bonding opportunities! Is there an easier way to seal a friendship than to give one another great justifications for buying the classic Fendi bag over the trendy one? Lunch or brunch—afterward or before—allows one to bask in the glow of her purchase or postulate about her shopping target for the day. Only a true friend will be able to dissect your proposed purchase with the same gusto that she uses to interpret last night's date.

Top Ten BAP Leisure Activities

1. Shopping
2. Saturday/Sunday brunch
3. Dim sum
4. Afternoon sangria and tapas/Sangria Sunday
5. Coffee talk at a coffee house
6. Concert in the park
7. People-watching
8. Restaurant hopping
9. Antiquing
10. Happy Hour during the week—it's not just for Fridays anymore!

To Cook or Not to Cook—Le BAP Chef

To cook or not to cook? That is the question. There are two types of culinary BAPs: Le BAP Chef and the Microwave Queen. The BAP who cooks is usually pretty savvy. She picks up tips from the Food Channel, creates her own recipes, and constantly gathers ideas for her next dinner party. Le BAP Chef never brags about her culinary skills—she doesn't want her boyfriend, or any friends for that matter, to expect her to cook all the time. Her best dish? Anything gourmet and chi-chi. Le BAP Chef's culinary contrast is blessed with the world's most advanced microwave and a Rolodex full of restaurants. Hey, the Zagat restaurant guide has nothing on the Microwave Queen! With an index finger callused from dialing for takeout, and kitchen cabinets overflowing with cereal and peanut butter and jelly, the Microwave Queen can frequently be found dining at Le BAP Chef's.

BAPs can be neatly divided into two categories. A BAP who. . . .

THROWS DOWN
Tries new restaurants to
find recipes

Owns All-Clad, Calphalon,
or Le Creuset

Makes B. Smith look like
a rank amateur

Emeril Lagasse calls her
for advice

Can plan and execute
a twelve-course meal in
a matter of minutes

Knows the difference
between basil and bok choy

TAKES OUT
Tries new restaurants out
of necessity

Owns Tupperware

Makes B. Smith rich

Tim and Nina Zagat call
her for advice

Can call a caterer in the
blink of an eye

Bok choy? Is that Chinese
for bad boys?

Martha Stewart
Martha Stewart Living
Dear Martha—

I am writing on paper I made myself to thank you for helping me out in a pinch. This year I was given the challenge of preparing Thanksgiving dinner for my family. To satisfy all palates I knew I'd have to reach back to my Georgia roots and make: macaroni and cheese, black-eyed peas, sweet potatoes, greens, chitlins, pecan pie, peach cobbler, and rolls. Frustrated and running out of time, I perused your cookbook as a last resort. Lo-and-behold, my meal as well as my decorations were on the pages before me.

I decorated my house in an Autumn theme, as you suggested, but I substituted kente cloth, that I weaved myself, rather than Irish linen to make my table runner, place mats, and trivets. To give the meal an overall Afrocentric theme, I made the table and chairs out of bamboo to simulate an African Chief's hut. Then I made koofis for each guest out of material scraps I'd saved for just such an occasion. But something still just didn't seem right . . . so I bought some beeswax, from the African arts and craft store, to roll perfect candles.

I picked the collards and sweet potatoes right out of my indoor garden, they were perfect for harvesting. The greens were flavored with just the right touch of smoked turkey, the sweet potatoes were wonderful with your special brown sugar glaze. The macaroni and cheese was perfectly baked, the black-eyed peas were tender and were tastefully flavored with bay leaves. Your chitlin infused foie gras was a hit, and the cranberry and orange dressing jazzed up my turkey just right.

I think you may have some competition
—Betty Betty
(aka—the Black Martha Stewart)

Buns, Abs, and Thighs

Having trouble getting to the gym, but still paying your monthly membership fee? Why not plunk down a few more dollars and get serious by hiring a personal trainer! Here's how to pick one:

- Get a referral from a friend
- Take a couple of classes. Is there a teacher that has an all-out good vibe? Grab 'em.
- If he's just plain fine, maybe you all can body double (i.e., so maybe you can do more than just work out together).

Fitness Wear

Let's face it, you may as well look good while you're working out . . . your future hubby could be checkin' you out!

What You'll Need:

1. Tons of great clothes that wick moisture away and keep you dry!
2. Got a great butt? Show it off. You're in the gym, for goodness sake, the one place you can wear Lycra and get away with it.
3. Tie those boobies down. You wouldn't want black eyes or sagging boobs before your time. Find a sports bra that works for you and wear it!
4. Splurge—if you like . . . there's plenty of designer workout gear and some of it's actually functional!
5. Socks—Thor-Lo it! By far the most comfortable socks out there.

Top BAP Fitness Activities

Cycling
Golf
In-line skating
Kickboxing
Lifting weights with her honey
Martial arts
Pilates
Spinning
Tennis
Urban rebounding
Yoga

One Nation Under a Groove—BAPs on the Rhythmic Art of Booty Shakin'

Between hair appointments, work, dating, and her daily dilemmas and duties, the BAP manages to shake her tail feather. Give a BAP any excuse to party and she will.

The Two-Step

Just as Parliament's "Flashlight" is the anthem for any child of the '60s, '70s, or '80s who grew up going to house parties, the two-step is the official BAP dance. Although most BAPs can dance, some are rhythmically challenged. The two-step, however, is nearly foolproof and universal among BAPs.

The basic two-step is a rhythmic movement stepping from one foot to the other while snapping your fingers or clapping your hands to the beat. BAPs bob their heads along with the beat and sometimes even add a little hip action. The whole objective of this dance is to look aloof and cute at the same time. The two-step is the fundamental dance because BAPs can schmooze, look good, and keep their hair under control all at once. It's all about priorities!

BAPs' PP (Personal Par-tay)

The doors close silently as she steps onto the elevator. Now the floor show begins. The foot taps, fingers snap, and her head bops to the beat. Her personal party is in full swing. Don't deny it, you've thrown a few of these yourself. No place is too sacred—the elevator, the car, even the shower. But the living room is the best place to really let loose. So, after a long day at work, with a hairbrush for a microphone, she puts on a one-woman show. The two-step, what's that? The Tootsie Roll, the Bankhead Bounce, the Butterfly—she tries them all. The party's over when she's exhausted or someone stops by.

Soulful Sounds

(All BAPs have at least ten from this list):

Personal Party (PP) Music

Chaka Khan
Jamiroquai
Madonna
Meshell Ndegeocello
Prince
Soul II Soul

Singers to Seduce By

Antonio Carlos Jobim
Brian McKnight
Cassandra Wilson

Diana Krall
Fourplay
Joe Sample
Loose Ends
Marcus Miller
Rachelle Ferrell
Sade
Sweetback
Vanessa Williams

Old-School Jams

Al Green
Barry White
Earth, Wind, and Fire
Isley Brothers
Michael Franks
Parliament
Stevie Wonder

Music Your Parents Listened to and Now You Can't Believe You Do, Too

Art Blakey
Chet Baker
Cole Porter
Dexter Gordon
Duke Ellington
Ella Fitzgerald
Frank Sinatra
Isaac Hayes
John Coltrane

Lou Rawls
Miles Davis
Ray Charles
Sarah Vaughan

Nouveau Soul

Amel Larrieux
Angie Stone
D'Angelo
Erykah Badu
Jill Scott
Lauryn Hill
Macy Gray
Maxwell
Rahsaan Patterson
Seal
The Brand New Heavies

Young Turks

Alana Davis
Des'ree
Dionne Farris
Kina
Les Nubiennes

Rapper's Delights

DMX
Dr. Dre
Eminem
Jay-Z

Nas
Nelly
Notorious B.I.G.
Snoop Dog (he's changed his name)
Tupac

Songs to Get Your God On

Andre Crouch
Fred Hammond
Hezekiah Walker
Kirk Franklin and The Family
Take 6
The Edwin Hawkins Singers
The Sounds of Blackness
The Winans
Yolanda Adams

Okay, I Admit It

Alanis Morissette
Billy Joel
Bruce Hornsby
Elton John
Elvis Costello
Joni Mitchell
Oasis
Sheryl Crow
The Beatles
The Eagles
The Grateful Dead
Van Morrison

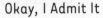

Lights, Camera, Soundtrack

Car Wash
Crooklyn
Disappearing Acts
Love and Basketball
Love Jones
Rent
Soul Food
The Best Man
The Wood
Waiting to Exhale

Music to Chill By

Art Porter
Carla Cook
David Sanborn
George Winston
Incognito
Jean Luc Ponty
Joshua Redman
Santana
Steely Dan

Vacation A-Go-Go

A BAP's wanderlust stems from her early travel experiences with her family. Seeing the world is a must for the BAP; her need to explore new vistas never abates! Bitten by the travel bug at an early age, vacations expose BAPs to various cultures and experiences. BAP vacations can be classified into three categories: relaxation, adventure, and education.

Relax, Relate, Release

Calm blue sea . . . the magical touch of a masseur releasing the kinks from her body . . . a moment to inhale and breathe fresh air. Every BAP needs a break from life's harsh realities. However, like everything else, the definition of relaxation is subject to interpretation. Betty's motto is work hard, play hard, and relax hard. Boho says "Boh-ring!" She opts for enrichment until her first spa massage, and then rationalizes how it fits into the spiritual scheme of things. Butterfly takes a bath every night for a week and she's just fine. And Bogus . . . well, it'll give her something to brag about.

Adventure

Adventure means different things to each BAP. The threat of a broken nail means adventure to Betty. Perfectly content to play it safe, Betty will reluctantly climb Mount Kilimanjaro—as long as she doesn't have to carry anything. No backpack could hold the gear for all of Boho's adventures. A canoe, mountain bike, or climbing equipment are the tools of her trade. Few eyebrows would be raised upon hearing that she broke bread with natives in a small Thai village. Butterflies and bungee jumping do not mix. Pay to ride a bike? Hurtle down the rapids? Climb a rock? Why? She'd rather use her money to see the Pyramids and the Pyrenées. Bogus? As long as it sounds good, like it was really amazing and something to be envious of, she'll do it. Who cares if she chickens out the moment the skydiving instructor says, "Jump!"

Education/Culture

No one will ever accuse a BAP of being an "Ugly American." When she's not on the beach, she's out among the people, soaking in the culture of her chosen vacation spot. BAPs are taught that the world is their oyster, so they must explore it. If the four B's planned a trip to Pompeii, it would be something like this: Betty would be anxious to see all the frescos she learned about in Art History 101. Boho would want to feel the presence of past spirits and of course enjoy a little *café au lait* with the locals. The BAPs wouldn't need to pay a tour guide because Butterfly would have read three different books on Pompeii in preparation. And Bogus? She's just traveling to impress. Each BAP would create her own experience. Being there is Bettier, living it is Bohomian, guiding it is Butterflyesque, and faking it is Bogus.

BAP Quiz #5

Match the BAP with her vacation:

1. Enjoys a weekend of window-shopping for the latest couture and *Prêt-à-porter* in Paris.
2. She's either rock climbing at Joshua Tree or skiing at Jackson Hole.
3. After a month on a photo safari in Africa, she heads off for a weekend of pampering.
4. A trip down South and then off to the Caribbean.

Answer Key:
1. Bogus   2. Boho   3. Betty   4. Butterfly.

I Spy with My Little Brown Eye

Top Spots to Spot BAPs

Two of the most popular summer vacation spots for African-Americans in the United States are Martha's Vineyard, Massachusetts, and Sag Harbor, New York.

Martha's Vineyard, Cape Cod, Massachusetts

While recently all the wrong sorts have converged on the island with their *très gauche* presence, the Vineyard still has a strong pull for the "in-crowd." Mainly an attraction for upper-crusty East Coasters or Midwesterners, the Vineyard offers a plethora of activities for people of all ages. BAP vacationers flock to Oak Bluffs, one of six enchanting towns on the island. Historically, this town is where African-American families over the generations have summered by the beach, played tennis, golfed, and watched each other's children grow up.

Sag Harbor, Long Island

Sag Harbor has been a popular destination for African-Americans since the turn of the century. Sag Harbor is only two and a half hours by train or seventy-five hours by car (oh, the Long Island Expressway!) from New York. Sag Harbor, a wholesome town located between Bridgehampton and East Hampton on Long Island, has always appealed to BAPs. There is a true sense of community among its residents. House parties are the rule, but do not show up unless you are a friend or at least a friend of a friend!

Honorable Mentions

Hilton Head, South Carolina

If you can get over the fact that the island is divided into plantations, then maybe you'll enjoy it. A mecca for FOB (if you have to ask, you aren't), policy wonks, and Tiger Woods wanna-bes, Hilton Head attracts the *crème de la crème*.

Union Pier, Michigan

For all those Midwesterners whose billable hours won't allow an extended stay on the Coast, a similar getaway exists right in their own backyard. Nicknamed the Martha's Vineyard of the Midwest, this quaint town (one and one-half hours east of Chicago and three hours from Detroit) provides a welcome respite from the great unwashed in the Midwest.

Fantastic Voyage

Is your ideal vacation a quiet bungalow in Fiji, or a V103 Caribbean Sunsplash with a thousand of your "closest" friends?

You Might Be on a Ghettoway If . . .

- Puffy is there.
- The official sponsor of the tennis tournament is a malt liquor company.
- Gold jewelry and Daisy Dukes are considered beachwear.
- Long-forgotten '70s groups are resurrected to play for the masses.
- Women parade through the hotel lobby in fur coats in July in Cancún.
- Guests pay their hotel bills in cash.

- Wake-up calls consist of one person yelling to another from the balcony.
- Folks sleep six to a room at the Ritz.
- There are hordes of 'Lil Kim look-alikes.

Jesus Loves Me, This I Know

Most BAPs grow up going to church regularly . . . then, they go away to college and only go to church when they're home visiting the 'rents . . . and then, they move out on their own and God takes a backseat to all of their more important objectives—work, shopping, exercise, and dating. But, oftentimes, when they hit thirty they realize that something is missing from their lives; could it be spirituality? Maybe they're feeling just plain lonely. Whatever the case, a song from childhood reemerges—"Jesus Loves Me, This I Know, for the Bible Tells Me So"—and the BAP hightails it back to the forgiving arms of the church.

You Know You're at a BAP Church If:

- The "right hand of fellowship" disrupts the church service because it turns into a social hour.
- The church elders frown when you walk in wearing slacks, or a skirt with no stockings.
- People join the church for the prestige of its name but never attend services.
- The woman who reads the announcements enunciates and projects as if she is performing at the Met.
- The Deacon Board's report reads like an SEC filing.
- The congregation knows better than to get "happy."
- The pastor's car is a foreign import.

The Fine Art of Looking Good While Do-Gooding: BAPs on Volunteerism

The BAPnation is built on three basic principles: achieving, giving, and shopping. Without a strong sense of volunteerism, her world would collapse. Some BAPs simply prefer to write a check, while others take a more hands-on approach. Each wants to contribute to the world in her own way—to somehow make it a better place.

Next to shopping, fund-raising and volunteerism come easily to Her Royal BAPness. For the hands-on BAP, a fund-raiser is just another excuse to plan a big party. The only difference is that at this one she'll be partying for a good cause. While others schlep around to gather generous donors, the fund-raising BAP merely lets her fingers do the walking. This is when her lifetime of attending exclusive schools and having memberships in elite clubs pays off. From the initial stages through the main event, the fund-raising BAP is where she has been her entire life, at the center of attention.

Thanks to the efforts of numerous BAPs nationwide, many organizations can count on substantial financial support from the African-American community.

Causes Célèbres

African American Civil War Memorial Freedom Foundation
AIDS Foundation
American Indian Heritage Foundation
Boys and Girls Clubs of America
Congressional Black Caucus Foundation
Girl Scouts Inc.
Habitat for Humanity
Hello Friend/Ennis William Cosby Foundation
National Breast Cancer Foundation

National Public Radio
Political Campaigns
Public Broadcasting System
Sickle Cell Anemia Research Foundation
The African-American Heritage Preservation Foundation
The American Red Cross
The Breast Cancer Research Foundation
The Jackie Robinson Foundation
The Jesse Owens Foundation
The Magic Johnson Foundation
The NAACP Legal Defense Fund
National Coalition of 100 Black Women
The National Urban League
The Thurgood Marshall Fund
UNICEF
United Negro College Fund
The 100 Black Men of America

Membership Is Priceless

Along with her birth certificate came her membership card to Jack and
Jill and the NAACP. Her college diploma is usually accompanied by a
sorority pin and eventually a Links invite. The ability to claim membership in exclusive organizations only serves to validate the BAP
lifestyle. Where else can Bogus flaunt her latest purchase or Betty network like crazy? The following groups are a touchstone for the platinum card–carrying BAP whose eternal motto is "Membership is
priceless."

The Links, Inc.

As the Black professional class came into prominence and leisure was no longer a dirty word, these upwardly mobile women came together to form the shining jewel in the crown of BAPdom—The Links, Inc. The Links, Inc. is the BAPs' equivalent of the Junior League.

The organization describes itself as "a group of friends committed to civic, educational, and cultural activities, with the singular purpose of serving community needs for the improvement of life and the pursuit of excellence." If you have to ask how to become a Link, your prospects of gaining admission are slim to none. Membership is by invitation only, so make sure to RSVP.

Several other womens organizations share similar outlooks:

The Girl Friends, Inc.

Only count on getting into this organization if you are a Betty or Boho. Membership is exclusive. Two members who know you well must sponsor you. You better get in on your first go around! If you're turned down for membership, that chapter is never allowed to propose your name again. The Girl Friends, Inc., is composed of forty chapters and includes approximately thirteen hundred members across the United States.

The Moles

The fun-loving BAP joins the Moles. This purely social organization makes no pretense of helping the community (BAPs' memberships in other organizations allow them to do that). No ifs, ands, or buts, they're all about partying. Founded by ten BAPs in 1928 in Norfolk, Virginia, to laugh, frolic, and party, they truly live by their motto: "Enjoy yourself, it's later than you think."

The Smart Set

Founded in 1937 by a group of schoolgirls headed off to college, the Smart Set's membership roster is another "Who's Who" in BAPdom. The organization performs some community service to justify its existence, but its main focus is socializing, being social, and staying social.

The Drifters

BAPs in Waco, Texas? Well, that's where the Drifters were founded in 1954. This organization focuses on charitable work and its members are extremely accomplished. But, then again, aren't all BAPs?

The Northeasterners

Founded in the 1930s by three sisters, the Northeasterners is an elite organization for BAPs. Be sure to befriend a Northeasterner, which will guarantee that you'll be invited to one of their lavish parties. Members, be wary of the Bogus—but why would she try to join, when she can eat, drink, and party at no cost?

Two Degrees of Separation: How to Play BAP Buddies
(TWO DEGREES OF SEPARATION + THE GREETING)/BAPDOM = BAP BUDDIES

Two Degrees of Separation . . . Well, Between Educated Black Folks

John Guare and Kevin Bacon perfected the theory of six degrees of separation—the concept that only six people separate each person in the world. But BAPs have pared down the degrees considerably. Put two BAPs in a room together who have never met before and within a matter of minutes they will have figured out who they know in common. And you'd better believe there's more than a tenuous connection between one of the BAPs and the common link. Fate? That may have something to do with it.

The Greeting—A Hug and a Kiss

It could happen anywhere—at a wedding, a party, in the mall, wherever she might bump into old friends. BAPs, females and males (yes, there are male counterparts) alike greet one another with a hug and a kiss on the cheek. But then again, there are those Kissing Kevins who insist on a kiss on the lips. These fellas mean no disrespect, in fact they consider the BAP to be a sister to them.

BAP Buddies—The Game

The BAP's social equation is based on two fundamental theorems: Who you know, and how you know them. These theorems are tested daily as BAPs throughout the country engage in friendly games of BAP Buddies. It can be played at any social gathering—from a chance meeting on the street to a cocktail party. When playing with someone you know, it's a game of catch-up. When playing with a stranger, you play to determine whom you know in common. BAPgirls start playing at an early age, and by the time they are grown they are well-versed in BAP Buddies.

How to Play

Your BAP status usually determines your game strategy. Betty engages in pleasant and genuine conversation, but typically holds her cards close to her chest unless of course she's in chat mode with a friend.

Boho on the other hand has nothing to hide and always has intriguing life experiences to share (recently returned from the Peace Corps, or quit her corporate job and teaches aerobics in Jamaica, or moved to LA to manage a friend's band). Butterfly . . . while she doesn't typically initiate the game, plays as if she cut her teeth at Jack and Jill conventions. Bogus generally tries to engage her buddy in a competitive round of one-upmanship, but Bettys, Bohos, and Butterflies wouldn't be caught dead engaging in such frivolity. A round of BAP Buddies often distinguishes the "lifers" from the neophytes.

A typical round of BAP Buddies will include some of the following questions:

1. Where do you live?
2. Where did you go to college?
3. What year did you graduate?
4. Where did you grow up?
5. What neighborhood?
6. Where did you go to lower, middle, and/or upper school?
7. Were you in Jack and Jill?
8. Did you go to the various professional conventions?
9. What do you do?
10. Where did your parents go to school?

Point System:

Find a buddy with one question:	25 points
Find a buddy with 2–4 questions:	10 points
Find a buddy with 5–7 questions:	5 points
Find a buddy with 8–10 questions:	1 point
Lie about who you know:	Automatic forfeit
Lie about where you went to school:	-25 points

Lie about what your parents do: -25 points
Lie about where you live: -25 points

The purpose of accumulating points is to maintain your card-carrying BAP status.

Globetrotting for Fun and Excitement: National BAP Events

Sure, folks across the nation gather together under the guise of some important career or sociopolitical event, but it's really all about shaking the groove thang! From the Congressional Black Caucus (CBC) weekend to the National Medical Association (NMA), BAPs converge in cities around the country to hobnob, network, and shop, of course!

Annually, a number of events attract the BAP masses from all corners of the country. Some are professional in nature while others strictly present an opportunity to revive *shakus groovethangus.* Networking. Socializing. Partying. The three go hand-in-hand.

Congressional Black Caucus Weekend

This is when the old adage "It's not what you know but who you know" comes to life. The annual CBC weekend is known as the premier gathering of African-American political, civic, and business leaders in the country. Some go for the cerebral discourse while others go to meet and greet. The purpose of the weekend is to set the political agenda for the upcoming year, and to have fun.

National Brotherhood of Skiers (NBS) Summit

If you ever want to know what a full-scale invasion is like, just go to the NBS summit for skiers and poseurs alike. Held biannually, BAPs converge on a town that never sees more than fifty Blacks in a ski season.

Skiing or faking the funk at the lodge represents a usual Summit day. When night falls, pale jaws are agape at the sight of eight thousand fashionably-clad soul skiers. Muzak is rapidly replaced by muzik—hip-hop, soul, and jazz. Folks just groove in their ski gear—boots and all. Providing the most entertainment are the Boguses, who can't ski a lick, but are decked out to their eyeballs in Bogner.

Black Enterprise/Pepsi Golf and Tennis Challenge

In a short period, the Black Enterprise/Pepsi Golf and Tennis Challenge has become one of the most influential national social gatherings of African-American professionals. Name any Black professional of power and you will be certain to hobnob with him or her at the BE Challenge. It has turned into quite a major event—like an amateur US Open and the Masters rolled into one. With golf, tennis, and spa days as the focus events, plenty of BAPs and admirers keep the festivities happening.

Various Professional Conventions

Although membership has its privileges, nonmember BAPs are welcome to attend conventions in their own cities. But leave it to the New York Bogus to show up in Los Angeles unannounced, uninvited, and uncredentialed. Some of the most notable conventions BAPs attend are: the National Black MBA Association, the National Bar Association, the National Medical Association, the National Dental Association, the National Society of Black Engineers, the National Association of Black Journalists, the National Association of Black Accountants, and the National Association of Black School Educators.

For Members Only

Every two years these organizations come together for a weekend of business, fun, and fellowship. Certain organizations are known far and wide for their spectacular conventions, particularly the Links, Sigma Pi Phi, and the Guardsmen.

BAPs on Books—A Reading List for the Well-Rounded BAP

A BAP who does not read is not a BAP . . .

Must-Haves. . . .

The Seven Secrets to Spiritual Success	Deepak Chopra
Acts of Faith	Iyanla Vanzant
All of E. Lynn Harris's books	
And We Are Not Saved	Derrick Bell
Bastard Out of Carolina	Dorothy Allison
Breakfast at Tiffany's	Truman Capote
Coffee Will Make You Black	April Sinclair
Good Hair	Benilde Little
How to Marry a Black Man	Mrs. Monique Jellerette deJongh and Mrs. Cassandra Marshall Cato-Louis

Invisible Man	Ralph Ellison
Mama Day	Gloria Naylor
Men Are from Mars, Women Are from Venus	John Gray
Native Son	Richard Wright
Rubyfruit Jungle	Rita Mae Brown
Sleeping in the Bed You Made	Virginia DeBerry and Donna Grant
Sweet Summer	Bebe Moore Campbell
The Blacker the Berry	Wallace Thurman
The Bluest Eye	Toni Morrison
The Color Purple	Alice Walker
The Easy Rawlins Series	Walter Mosley
The God of Small Things	Arundhati Roy
The Wedding	Dorothy West
The Women's Room	Marilyn French
Their Eyes Were Watching God	Zora Neale Hurston
What Looks Like Crazy on an Ordinary Day	Pearl Cleage
The Divine Secrets of the Ya-Ya Sisterhood	Rebecca Wells

Collection Additions—Aspire to Add These to Your Collection

A Piece of Mine	J. California Cooper
Memoirs of a Geisha	Arthur Golden
A Widow for One Year	John Irving
Brothers and Sisters	Bebe Moore Campbell
Clover	Dori Sanders
Cold Sassy Tree	Olive Ann Burns
Innocents Abroad	Mark Twain
Kindred	Octavia Butler
Krik? Krak!	Edwidge Danticat
Possessing the Secret of Joy	Alice Walker

The Hours   Michael Cunningham
The Interpreter of Maladies   Jhumpa Lahiri
The Rapture of Canaan   Sherri Reynolds
The Song of Solomon   Toni Morrison
Waiting to Exhale   Terry McMillan
White Teeth   Zadie Smith
Anything by:
Chinua Achebe
Maya Angelou
James Baldwin
Deepak Chopra
William Faulkner
Henry Louis Gates
Graham Greene
Zora Neal Hurston
John Irving
Toni Morrison
Gloria Naylor
Amy Tan
Cornell West
Richard Wright

Favorite BAP Websites

www.africana.com
www.amistad.org
www.aol.com
www.amazon.com
www.Askjeeves.com
www.Bananarepublic.com
www.Barnesandnoble.com
www.bet.com
www.blackexpressions.com
www.blackvoices.com
www.Bluefly.com
www.Cartier.com
www.dailycandy.com
www.Drugstore.com
www.Ebay.com
www.Ehow.com
www.Elle.com
www.Eluxury.com
www.estyle.com

www.Etrade.com
www.everythingblack.com
www.expedia.com
www.Gentlehints.com
www.google.com
www.netnoir.com
www.Neimanmarcus.com
www.oprah.com
www.Redenvelope.com
www.Sephora.com
www.shesheme.com
www.style.com
www.Styleshop.com
www.Thestreet.com
www.tiffany.com
www.Travelocity.com
www.twotightshoes.net
www.ubid.com
www.Webmd.com

HERE COMES THE BRIDE

BAP dating—the team sport—eventually culminates with a lasting love as the trophy. BAParents sent her to the right schools and camps and she joined the right organizations all in the hopes of finding her perfect mate. And finally here it is . . . the Big Day. BAPmoms go crazy, BAPdads get hazy, and the fiancé is just plain lazy. Big or small, casual or formal, at the Ritz or a Buddhist temple, BAP weddings are varied. But, the underlying theme is perfection.

I Can't Believe This Is Happening . . .

She's thought of everything—the bridal gown, the bridesmaids, flower girls, five-tiered cakes, the Wedgwood pattern, honeymoon in Tuscany, and the jazz quartet for the reception . . . just one minor detail is missing—the groom! (BAP Note: If you have not been thinking about this day, planning the music you want played, your bridal party, and so on, go back to the beginning and take the BAP Test to determine your BAP status.) The BAP has a dilemma—how to choose between Mr. Right and Mr. Alright. Both men are accomplished and handsome, but one falls just short. Who will the lucky guy be?

ANTHONY	SPENCER
Ht 6'2" Wt 180	Ht 5'11" Wt 170
Dark and dashing—Is often asked, "Are you Morris Chestnut?"	Brown and beautiful— A Larenz Tate look-alike

Background: Washington, D.C. St. Albans alum Williams College Harvard Business School	Background: Shaker Heights, Ohio Shaker Heights High Indiana University Kellogg School of Business
Career: Two years at Morgan Stanley; currently a VP at Goldman	Career: Regional sales director, Eli Lilly Pharmaceuticals
Home: New York, NY	Home: Indianapolis, IN
Frat: Kappa Alpha Psi	Frat: GDI
Other: Golf addict; avid reader of *Forbes* and the *Industry Standard*; great abs; pioneering an Internet start-up	Other: Cooking; bowling; a smile to die for
Wardrobe: Zegna and Banana	Wardrobe: Brooks Brothers and The Gap
Favorite Musician: John Coltrane	Favorite Musician: Miles Davis
Favorite Group: Tribe Called Quest	Favorite Group: The Roots
Last Book Read: *Tuesdays with Morrie*	Last Book Read: *Investment Tips for Dummies*
Theory on Jewelry Shopping: Understands the importance of the little blue box	Theory on Jewelry Shopping: Blue what?

While both men seem like great catches, one is slightly more appealing to the BAP. Anthony currently lives in New York, while Spencer is stuck in Indianapolis—what BAP would move to Indiana? Spencer just read *Investment Tips for Dummies* (the BAP can't take care of money, and he can't either?). Spencer could also use some style lessons. Although he may not shop at Tiffany's, Spencer should know about the blue box. Spencer is a good catch, to be sure; Anthony is just a better one.

And You Thought Honey-dos Were Melons?

Honey, will you help me zip my dress?
Honey, will you walk the dog?
Honey, will you run to the drugstore and pick up some tampons?

The list is endless, but the question always begins with "Honey, will you . . ." The boyfriend who quietly assents to the wishes of his beloved BAP's "Honey, will you . . ." (Honey, will you do this; Honey, will you do that) is a perfect honey-do ripe for marrying. Human to a fault, he may disappoint his beloved by failing to follow through on her every honey-do request, but this doesn't mean he loves his BAP any less.

Is Your Honey-do Unripe?

Here are a few gardening tips to cultivate your unripe melon:

1. Show him lots of affection.
2. Let him feel like he's in charge.
3. Only ask for small requests initially, and then lead up to bigger things.

Not Your Type? Could Be Mr. Right

Ian: I fell in love with Betty the moment I saw her walking toward me. I just felt some sort of kismet or karma; something said to me, "This is the woman I'm going to marry." She was the most beautiful woman I'd ever seen—she moved so confidently and was just perfect.

Betty: Ian seemed really nice. He wasn't my type, though. I couldn't get Mr. Right Now out of my mind. He was soooo fine. Unfortunately, Mr. Right Now wasn't bringing too much to the table, but his good looks . . . I began to think I should pay attention to Ian; he could be Mr. Right.

BAP Quiz #6

Each of the four BAPs dreams of her wedding day. What strategy does each employ to meet that perfect man?

1. She prays each night for the perfect man.
2. She dates until she drops.
3. She casually goes out until someone catches her fancy.
4. Thumbs through *Ebony*'s most eligible bachelors and finds the one with the largest balance sheet.

Answer Key:
1. Butterfly   2. Betty   3. Boho   4. Bogus.

The Proposal

Can't believe he's going to propose? Where he'll do it . . . no one knows. To keep him from doing it while his boys are in tow, check out the following list of great places:

1. On a carriage ride
2. On vacation—preferably Paris, the Caribbean, or some other exotic/romantic locale
3. In a park
4. In the dark . . . just kidding
5. At the beach
6. On the slopes
7. Atop Mount Hope
8. Almost anywhere as long as he gets down on one knee and has an acceptable ring

Big . . . Bigger . . . Biggest . . . the Ring

Sure, we were all taught that size doesn't matter, but tell that to the poor BAP holding back tears of sadness when she opens the Zales box with an even smaller diamond inside. If he wants you, he has to show it, one carat at a time! Carol Channing had it right—diamonds are a girl's best friend, and a BAP's too!

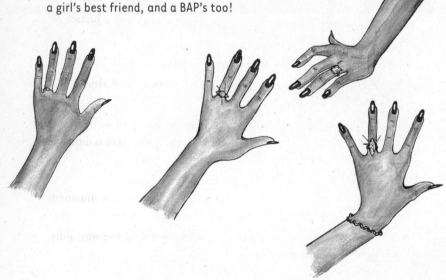

How to Determine the Depth (Weight and Clarity) of His Love for You

Look at your hand and your sweetie's bank account. And what you don't know will hurt you, so take the time to find out what vs1 and all the rest of the lingo stands for.

CARATS	CLARITY	COMMENTS
.5–1	low-med	It's April Fools', right?
	high	You're just friends—special dispensation if he's just starting out.
1–2	low-med	Fine for now . . . you can always upgrade next year.
	high	He's the man!
2–4	low-med	Is it in a little blue box?
	high	He must be crazy in love . . .
4 and up	low-med	Bogus, you've found your match!
	high	Once you regain your vision, find a justice of the peace!

Dreams of Harry Winston Diamonds Dance in Her Head

While BAPs have the Four P's, diamonds have the Four C's. They were made for one another! Here are the key things that make a diamond as beautiful as a BAP.

Cut—determines how much it shines, shines, shines.

Color—Easy, the less color the better. But those yellow diamonds are still gorgeous!

Carats—Not the ones Bugs Bunny is in love with! By the way, girls, bigger is not always better!

Clarity—How flawed are you? Well, sometimes a diamond is, too! The following ratings explain just how much.

Rating	What It Means to Her
FL—Flawless	Perfect baby!
VVS—Very very slight inclusions	A little less perfect.
VS—Very slight inclusions	A little more less perfect.
SI—Slight inclusions	Cloudy with thunderstorms! Where no BAP will go. Tiffany's doesn't even think about these.

The UnDiamond

So diamonds aren't your best friend? Give these beautiful colored gemstones a try. The traditional choice of European royalty, surely they're good enough for her royal highness, the BAP. And each one has special meaning to boot!

Sapphire—Blue—Sincerity
Ruby—Red—Passion
Emerald—Green—Love and Fertility

BAP Quiz #7

A BAP's fiancé gives her a two-carat vvs engagement ring. How does she respond?

1. We could donate money to a charity instead of my wearing this, but it is beautiful.
2. I'm speechless, it takes my breath away.
3. I told you I wanted a BIG ring.
4. Baby, you didn't have to do this.

Answer Key:

1. Boho   2. Betty   3. Bogus   4. Butterfly.

Tales from the Altar

Something Borrowed, Something Blue . . . I Know What I'm Wearing, How About You?

"Isn't she lovely!" That's what the BAP wants to hear as she's walking down the aisle in the dress that she's pictured her entire life. Perfect wedding gowns have one thing in common—the power to make any bride beautiful. The wedding dress sets the tone, mood, and budget of the event—wracking nerves and busting budgets in its mad dash towards matrimony.

Betty—She's in a class all her own in this category. She's on a Holy Grail-like quest for that perfect dress. No effort is too great, no store too far, in the search of that special frock.

Boho—Being eclectic, she can't be bothered with all that drama. If she's going to Paris to find a dress, it's only after she completes her art classes at the Sorbonne.

Butterfly—Like Betty, Butterfly is serious about her tasks. So serious, that if you get in her way you might draw back a nub. Her wedding is a very special event, like a sweet sixteen, a cotillion, and graduation all rolled into one.

Bogus—Well, suffice it to say that she puts the ding-a-ling in wedding. Her dress is all bells and whistles. Silk organza is not expensive enough! Hand-sewn glass beads from Italy—but only if a detailed description of the handiwork is printed in the wedding program.

Instant Message
From: mrsbetty@crazyBAPmom.com
To: betty@bridetobe.com
Subject: Yet another schedule

Hi Dear,
Just got a call from Dayton's . . . here's the schedule for the weekend:

Saturday: 10 A.M.	Carolina Herrera Trunk Show
Saturday: 1:30 P.M.	Dayton's
Sunday: 12 noon	Wedding Chapel
Sunday: 2:30 P.M.	Bridal Center

No apptmts, go if time:
Angelique's
Bridal Accents

Talk to you later . . . Came across a great musician for you guys to meet . . . Really impressed by his credentials!
Love, Mom

Instant Message
From: mrsbetty@crazyBAPmom.com
To: betty@bridetobe.com
Subject: Revised Schedule

Ignore my previous e-mail. Here's the new schedule:

Saturday: 10 A.M.	Vera Wang Trunk Show
Saturday: 1:30 P.M.	Saks Bridal Salon
Saturday: 3:30 P.M.	The Ultimate Bride
Saturday: 7:30 P.M.	La Bella Sposa
Sunday: 12 noon	Wedding Chapel
Sunday: 2:30 P.M.	Exclusives for the Bride

No apptmts, go if time (Ha Ha!):
Bargain Bridal
Loehman's
Love, Mom

Don't let the search for the perfect dress escalate to a Battle of the BAPfamily.

Advice to BAPs	Advice to BAPmoms	Advice to BAPdads
1. Go on your first appointment without Mom to narrow down your choices.	1. Don't force or even suggest that your daughter wear your dress.	1. Remember . . . you'll do anything to keep your princess happy.
2. Don't embarrass your mother in public.	2. It's your daughter's wedding, not yours.	2. They may ask for your advice, but don't fall into their trap—they don't really want it.
3. If all else fails, tears still work.	3. Can't you ease up for once?	3. Just smile, smile, smile.

Instant Message
From: atruebetty@tatoo.com
To: ysmallwood@maidofhonor.com
Subject: The Secret's Out

Okay—I can't believe this. Mom and I found the absolute perfect dress on our third weekend of shopping! The bad thing—Mom's not talking to me. She finally saw the tattoo! I completely forgot to hide it because I was so excited about the DRESS! What a mess!!!!! She passed out in the bridal shop and when she came to—well, let's just say she suggested laser surgery to remove it. So I got a beautiful Vera Wang dress—but the Secret is out!

Friends Don't Let Friends Become Bridesmaids

Who ever thought that saddling ten women with ill-fitting, pastel, floral dresses and matching dyed pumps is a sign of friendship? Sure you're ecstatic for your girl—she's finally going to jump the broom. But do you really have to wear *that?* It's bad enough that the bride is bankrupting you, but does she have to make you look like the Bridesmaid of Frankenstein, too?!!

Who Said I Wanted to be a Bridesmaid Anyway?
- Not with those hideous dresses
- Not if I have to do all of your dirty work
- Not if I have to deal with a neurotic bride
- Not if those shoes will give me corns
- Not if there aren't any eligible groomsmen

Instant Message
From: bboho@lastlaugh.com
To: megan@workaholic.com
Subject: Mimi's Wedding

You missed it! I thought Mimi was going to call the wedding off ten minutes beforehand . . . we got out of the limo at the church and Paul was standing in the foyer with a powder blue '70s tuxedo on— ruffled shirt and all. If nothing else, it gave the bridal party a great laugh after all the grief she put us through. You know Mimi—drama queen that she is. . . . Can't take a joke. . . . A look of horror, then tears! (But for the full church, the last laugh could have been on him if she'd left him standing at the altar alone.)

The BAP Bridesmaid Pact

If Brides and Bridesmaids were to draw up a contract before the Big Day, it might look something like this.

I, _____ (the bridesmaid's name), best, oldest, college roomie, friend, relative (circle one) of _____ (bride's name), hereby witness and affix my signature to this bridesmaid's agreement.

For good and valuable consideration, the bridesmaid agrees to purchase one putrid, hideous, ungodly (circle one) bridesmaid outfit that is to the sole liking of the bride. Said Bridesmaid also agrees to perform such additional services, at great financial cost to herself only, as (i) stuffing invites with gloves so as not to smudge the ink, (ii) accompanying the bride to dress fittings, (iii) planning the bridal shower, and/or (iv) organizing the spa weekend Bachelorette Party.

I, _____, do promise and agree to spend 30 percent or more of my net or gross income, whichever is greater, on a plethora of gifts, travel, and any other wedding related activities as the bride sees fit.

WHEREAS, I am of unsound mind and body, I hereby affix my signature to this pledge of our friendship and loyalty.

[Signed]
I Must Be Crazy

No BAPbride Would Ever . . .

1. Require her bridesmaids to use a professional makeup artist but ask them to pay for it themselves.
2. Expect that only the "most gainfully employed" bridesmaids should host and pay for her bridal shower.
3. Ask her bridesmaids to be in her wedding and purchase their dresses prior to her officially being engaged.
4. Send her bridesmaids to a hairdresser who has them walking down the aisle looking like Sha-Nay-Nay.
5. Brag about the size and cost of her ring (being excited and bragging are two different things).
6. Promise her bridesmaids that they could definitely wear their bridesmaid dresses again (we all know that's a lie).
7. Elope (if by some chance she did, she'd only tell her best friend and still have the wedding her mother always dreamed of).
8. Walk down the aisle visibly pregnant.
9. Let it be known there are three guest lists.

Matrimonial Maternal Admonitions

1. You're his responsibility now—thank God.
2. If you keep your house like you kept your room—don't expect to keep your man.
3. Remember . . . mortgage payments before shopping sprees.

4. (For Boho) Something borrowed does not include belly-button rings.
5. I hope you had a good time because I'm not doing this again.

Goin' to the Chapel

Six Months or More Ahead

1. *No bullhorn? An announcement in the paper will do.*
   No cheesy frosted photos, please!
2. *Haul out the Brinks truck but don't forget the budget.*
   A budget? New word to the BAP. She'll leave this step to her father after ensuring that he understands her priorities: an Escada wedding dress. . . .
3. *Hire a bridal consultant.*
   A professional one, not your next-door neighbor who promises to save you a bundle.
4. *Pick a spot, any spot . . . well, not any spot.*
   Halls are out. Private clubs, estates, and hotels are in. Book them fast. You aren't the only BAP getting married this year. Hint: Look for a site that has character, it will minimize your need to decorate—elegantly simple is best.
5. *Guess who's coming to dinner—the guest list.*
   Should be shorter than *War and Peace* and more diverse than the Supreme Court. The biggest challenge of the wedding? Your family and his. The parents' friends (they're important, they "give good gifts"). You and your fiancé's friends. The list will be re-

vised and revised just short of blood being drawn. Don't invite the world. Remember, you're planning your wedding, not a pageant.

6. *Less is more—choosing your attendants.*
   Again, remember that this is a wedding, not the Macy's Thanksgiving Day parade. Keep the chorus line to a minimum.

7. *Order dress and accessories including veil, gloves, and shoes.*
   No same-day searching for this event. If you're lucky it will take you and your mother only two to three years to come to a mutual decision on your dress.

Four to Six Months Ahead

1. *Bon appetit—choosing a caterer.*
   We'll say it once . . . no rubber chicken.

2. *Smile for the camera—book photographer and videographer.*
   Find someone who knows the difference between Pentax and Anthrax. Color, black-and-white, or both will do. You make the call.

3. *You choose, they buy—register for gifts.*
   Shopping without having to pay . . . it's like a dream come true!

4. *Musique, muzak, or musik—booking musicians for reception.*
   Remember, your guests are attending a wedding, not a symphony.

5. *Mind your manners, check with Emily—invites and Thank-You notes.*
   You may need to brush up on your Emily Post. No need for titles, and that means neither his nor yours. And remember, engraving and laser printing are two very different things.

6. *The added touch—booking a calligrapher.*
   Using a metallic pen does not make someone a calligrapher.

7. *Keeping it simple—choosing wedding favors.*

An awful tradition—no matter how hard you try, they always end up cheesy.

Two to Four Months

1. *No kissing cousins—take the blood test.*
   Make sure you're not marrying your cousin.
2. *Meet the man or woman—discuss the service with the officiant.*
   Remember, it's a wedding, not an extravaganza.
3. *Last chance—the final dress-fitting.*
   Hope you lost all the weight you wanted to by now. No more late-night Ben & Jerry's binges.
4. *Love and poetry go hand in hand—choosing readings for ceremony.*
   Choose a friend who can read with feeling and without bursting into tears!
5. *Writing your own vows? Do so now!*
   From the heart . . . not from a book.
6. *With this ring—buy the wedding bands.*
   To match or not to match is the question. Whatever you choose, make it simple; remember, you'll be wearing it every day for the rest of your life.

One to Two Months Ahead

1. *Playbill—have programs printed.*
   This is not an advertisement . . . no need to list everyone involved in the wedding from the florist to the dress designer.
2. *To hyphenate or not—changing your name.*
   If his name doesn't work with what you've got . . . keep yours.
3. *Mr. Postman—mail invitations.*
   Make sure you've spelled your guests' names correctly.

4. *Stop pretending you don't live together—send out change of address information.*
   Since the perfect princess never shacks up, let everyone know where and when you'll be moving.
5. *Get it right—practice hairstyle with headpiece.*
   Your stylist must assist you. Look for tips to reduce the frizz factor. You wouldn't want to look like a peacock on your Big Day.
6. *Get down and boogie—the bachelorette party.*
   Go wild (not buck wild) and enjoy.

One Week Before

1. *Fly me to the moon—pack bag for honeymoon.*
   One bag maximum.
2. *Today is all about you—enjoy a facial or other beauty treatment(s).*
   Any excuse to pamper yourself.

One Day Ahead

1. *Pray.*
2. *Pray.*
3. *Pray.*

The Wedding Day

1. *Enjoy.*
2. *Enjoy.*
3. *Enjoy.*

Top Shops for a BAPregistry

Williams Sonoma	For serious cooks
Crate & Barrel	For all of the basics and furniture too
Tiffany & Co.	For the finer things. . . .
Restoration Hardware	Knickknacks and clickety-clacks
Gumps	A San Fran staple
Neiman Marcus /	For extraordinarily beautiful
Bergdorf Goodman	things
Local Department Stores	Anything you couldn't get at Crate or Tiffany's
Pottery Barn	Basics with style
Weddings.com	Have no fear, Internet registering is here
Bloomies	For Big Brown Bags of gifts
Barney's	Fun and funky housewares

	BETTY	BOHO	BUTTERFLY	BOGUS
The Ring	Platinum round brilliant from Tiffany's	Platinum emerald cut (emerald stone)	White gold round brilliant	4 carat low quality Marquis
The Bride Wore	Vera Wang	Cynthia Rowley	Her mother's wedding gown	Tommy Hilfiger
When and Where	Rockefeller Chapel, Chicago; Reception at her Dad's club; Fall Wedding (no frizz factor)	Cumberland Island, GA; On the beach; Springtime	Abyssinian Baptist Church, New York, New York; Reception at the church hall; August bride	The Beverly Hills Hilton; June, of course
The Bridesmaids Wore	Vera Wang Bridesmaids	Badgley Mishka; Asian-theme dresses with thongs	A dress you can never wear again	A sabotage dress (so nobody would look better than the bride)
The Music	Cocktail Hour: Jazz ensemble Reception: Band used for all BAP events	Cocktail Hour: Tuck and Patti Reception: Live band	Deejay	Musical stylings of Puff Daddy
The Menu	Choice of Lamb, Chicken, or Salmon	Gourmet Caribbean	Buffet	Expensive cake—beautiful on the outside, dried out, over-done on the inside
First Dance	Louie Armstrong's "What a Wonderful World"	Antonio Carlos Jobim's "The Wave"	Nat King Cole's "Unforget-table"	Chaka Khan's "I'm Every Woman"

Instant Message
From: mrsbetty@crazyBAPmom.com
To: betty@bridetobe.com
Subject: Schedule for 1/28-30/01

Can't wait to see you this weekend.

    Okay . . . now here's what we have set up at the moment:

Friday:

9:45 A.M.	Radisson Plaza
11:30 A.M.	Four Seasons
1:00 P.M.	Michael Anderson, Photographer
3:30 P.M.	Portrait Gallery, Steve Larson
Saturday:	
9:30 A.M.	Larkspur, floral design specialist
2:30 P.M.	The Perfect Wedding, wedding consultant
6:00 P.M.	Carmen's wedding (let's check it out)
Sunday:	
10:00 A.M.	Tutti Fiori, florist

Let me know what you and John think . . . Obviously we have to choose the site now. The photographer and florist book early, so if we see something we like, we need to make the selection now. Dad talked to the wedding coordinator on Sunday, and she has e-mailed her credentials to me. I like the idea of having her help, especially on the day of the wedding to oversee all of the activities and arrangements. Plus, she knows and has worked with many suppliers and has suggestions on whom to contact. She has suggested a fantastic group of violinists who have a McPhail Music Center background. She wants to meet you and John so she can have firsthand input from you, hence the Satur-

---

day visit at our house. Have a great day . . . Hope my work is appreciated!!!! Love, Mom :)

The Traditional Girl in a High-Tech World

Does the Internet at a BAP's wedding sound a bit contradictory? Well, forget about contradiction . . . you'll just have to buck tradition here. Don't miss out. Wedding sites now do everything from designing your engagement ring and e-mailing it to your honey to registering you for everything without you having to pay any money up front! Check out a few of these wedding sites, guaranteed to make your life easier.
www.weddings.com
www.TheKnot.com
www.adiamondisforever.com
www.bridesofcolor.com

All Groomed Out . . . The Best of Tuxedos

Make sure your honey looks as yummy as you. Don't forget it's The Big Day for both of you—make sure he looks his best, too! A tuxedo's cut is everything, so have him try these on for size:

Brioni
Hugo Boss
Giorgio Armani
Ralph Lauren Purple Label
Zegna
Oxford

The BAP's Big Day

What to Do with Your Country Cousins

Most BAPs can trace their roots back to quiet hamlets in the South. Summer forays to those ancient stomping grounds are sweet, dream-like memories. But the other side of the dream is a nightmare, like Uncle Willie who has an unwavering faith that sucking on a toothpick and wearing Stacy Adams are surefire lady-killers, or Auntie SuSu who insists that chitterlings are acceptable wedding dinner fare. Let's not forget your cousins BeBe and Cookie, whose antics are sure to show you up. What is a BAP to do?

Solutions to the Country Cousin Problem

Appoint a strapping groomsman to hide the Tupperware bowl full of ham hocks and neck bones that suddenly appears on the buffet table, and:

- Remind them not to bring their house shoes with them to the reception.
- Hire a bodyguard (in case an old family feud flares up).
- Have a satellite reception/special invite only luncheon.
- Say they are the entertainment.
- Accept your family as they are—just have fun.

You Know It's a Betty Wedding If . . .

- Her "status" guests are all old family friends.
- She flew her bridesmaids to Negril, Jamaica, for some fun in the sun.
- Her wedding is profiled in *Town & Country*.

You Know It's a Boho Wedding If . . .

- Shoes are optional.
- There are wedding cupcakes.
- The ceremony takes place on a beach.

You Know It's a Butterfly Wedding If . . .

- There's a chitterlings and ham hock table.
- Her bridesmaids are wearing fishnet stockings.
- Her cousin Nini sings "I Believe I Can Fly."
- She insists on marching down the aisle to her favorite R&B love song.

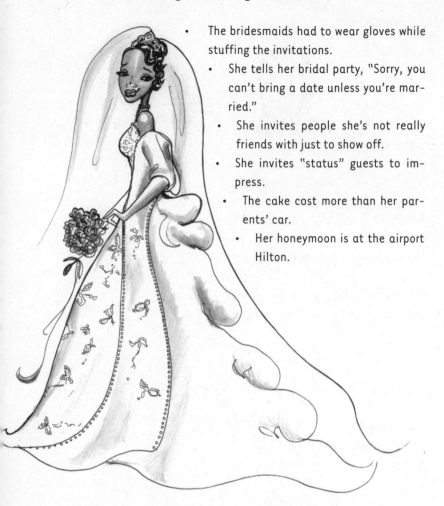

- The bridesmaids had to wear gloves while stuffing the invitations.
  - She tells her bridal party, "Sorry, you can't bring a date unless you're married."
  - She invites people she's not really friends with just to show off.
  - She invites "status" guests to impress.
  - The cake cost more than her parents' car.
  - Her honeymoon is at the airport Hilton.

Bridal Boo-Boos

- Performing relatives
- Doing your own hair and makeup
- Using your cousin's friend's limo service
- Not ordering enough food
- Cash bar

Paternal Admonitions

- You'll always be my little girl.
- You have to give me my Amex card back. Now!
- It took a little bit longer than I thought.

Top BAP Honeymoon Spots

1. Italy—Verona, Venice, anywhere in Tuscany
2. The South Pacific—Bora-Bora, Bali, Tahiti
3. St. Barth's
4. The Greek Islands
5. St. Lucia
6. Hawaii—Maui
7. Paris
8. Spain
9. Portugal
10. Whistler—Alberta, Canada

The Baby Carriage

First comes love, then comes marriage, then comes Baby BAP in the baby carriage. The cycle repeats itself and yet another precious little girl enters into the ranks of the many, the proud, the BAPs!

ESSENTIAL BAP FACTS

The BAP in Training

The American Tennis Association
William H. G. Fitzgerald Tennis Center
16th and Kennedy Streets NW, Washington, DC
(202) 291–9893

   Tennis is unique in that a national organization for African-Americans exists. In addition to the United States Tennis Association, many BAPs are members of the American Tennis Association (ATA), the oldest African-American sports association in the United States. Founded in 1916, the ATA is an integral part of the African-American tennis community. The ATA sponsors local tournaments throughout the country. Its annual national tournament is held in August. It is the social event of the summer, not to be missed by avid tennis players.

Minority Golf Association of America, Inc.
P.O. Box 1081 ~ Westhampton Beach, NY 11978
(631) 288–8255

   The MGAA is a nonprofit 501(C)(3) organization devoted to introducing young people to golf as a social, business, and employment opportunity.

The National Brotherhood of Skiers
National Headquarters
1525 E. 53rd Street, Suite 408
Chicago, IL 60615
(773) 955–4100

Major cities have ski clubs where the BAPgirl can ski on the weekends. Through the Snow Gophers in Chicago, the Jim Dandy Ski Club in Detroit, the Sno-Burners in New York, and the Four Seasons West in Los Angeles, BAPs fellowship with their snow-loving brethren with nary a nap out of place!

NBS is the largest and oldest ski organization for African-Americans in the United States. Founded in 1974 to nurture snow sports among African-Americans, the NBS has grown to an organization with over 14,000 members in over 81 ski clubs throughout the country. The only event of its kind, the NBS Summit, attracts African-Americans of all ages from all parts of the country.

Jack and Jill of America, Inc.

Jack and Jill of America, Inc., was founded in 1938 by twelve affluent African-American Philadelphia mothers as a play group for their children. Today, Jack and Jill has over 220 chapters and 8,000 members across the United States and Germany. From toddlers to high school seniors, members take part in well-orchestrated activities. Why, members even have to participate in public service activities each year! Doesn't this show what regular "elitist" folks they are? As high school draws to a close, so does active participation in Jack and Jill. Yet the friendships last a lifetime.

Hot Fun in the Summertime
Australia: Rainforest to Reef
Program Coordinators
P.O. Box 3149

Ashland, OR 97520
(888) 477–7620

A coed residential community service and cultural program for high school students. Program focus includes rain forest ecology, reefs, Aboriginal culture, and marine biology.

Camp Atwater
c/o Urban League of Springfield, Inc.
756 State Street
Springfield, MA 01109
(413) 739–7211

The oldest and most well-known Black camp is Camp Atwater in North Brookfield, Massachusetts.

The Children's International Summer Villages
CISV USA National Office
1375 Kemper Meadow Drive, Suite 9-H
Cincinnati, OH 45240
(888) CISV–USA

CISV is an independent, nonpolitical volunteer organization promoting peace, education, and cross-cultural friendship. CISV programs are based on the premise that there is hope for the future and that actions of individuals can and do have significance in community, national, and international affairs. Emphasizing friendship, CISV educates through action, stressing cooperation rather than competition in activities based upon organizational goals of inspirational and educational value.

INROADS, Inc.
10 South Broadway, Suite 700
St. Louis, MO 63102
(314) 241–7488

    A national program to develop and place talented minority youth in business and industry and prepare them for corporate and community leadership.

MPS Summer Challenge
Miss Porter's School
60 Main Street
Farmington, CT 06032
(860) 409–3692

    A four-week summer boarding program for girls entering grades seven through nine featuring mathematics, science and technology, sports, self-defense, field trips, and recreation.

OxBridge Academic Programs
Cathedral Station
P.O. Box 1001
New York, NY 10025
(800) 828–8349

    Academic summer programs at Oxford and Cambridge Universities in England and in the heart of Paris. A wide range of courses in the humanities, social sciences, and creative arts for boys and girls grades eight through twelve.

People to People Student Ambassador Programs
National Director
Dwight D. Eisenhower Building
Spokane, WA 99202
(509) 534–0430
   Cultural exchange and international awareness program for children ages eleven through eighteen. Includes travel in Italy, New Zealand, and South Africa.

Wellesley College Exploration Program
Exploration Summer Programs
470 Washington Street
P.O. Box 368
Norwood, MA 02062
(781) 762–7400
   A balanced precollege experience including academic enrichment workshops, college level seminars, and athletic, artistic, and recreational activities.

To Go to College or Not to Go to College?

Alpha Kappa Alpha Sorority, Inc.
5656 South Stony Island Avenue
Chicago, IL 60637
(773) 684–1282
   Alpha Kappa Alpha Sorority, Inc., is the nation's oldest African-American sorority and community service organization. Sixteen women at Howard University founded the sorority in 1908. Today the organization includes over 140,000 members nationally and internationally.

Delta Sigma Theta Sorority, Inc.
1707 New Hampshire Avenue NW
Washington, DC 20009
(202) 986–2400

Delta Sigma Theta Sorority, Inc., is the second oldest and largest African-American sorority. Founded in 1913 by twenty-two women at Howard University, Delta Sigma Theta has more than 190,000 members in more than 870 chapters internationally.

The Good Life: The BAP All Grown Up

Vacation A-Go-Go
Martha's Vineyard

African-Americans have vacationed on Martha's Vineyard since the early 1900s. The Vineyard is a one-hundred-square-mile island located off Cape Cod, Massachusetts. Be sure to visit the following African-American–owned businesses:

- *Twin Oaks Inn*
  P.O. Box 1767
  20 Edgartown Road
  Vineyard Haven, MA 02568–1767
  (800) 696–8633
  The Dutch colonial–style house was built in 1906 and has a delightful wraparound enclosed front porch with antique wicker furniture. Twin Oaks Inn was awarded the 1996 Crème de la Crème Award from *Boston Best Guide* for "Best Atmosphere."
- *Cousen Rose's Art Gallery*
  Great selection of African-American art and book signings of notable African-American authors.

- *Summer Breeze Gift Shop*
  If you're looking for linens, candles, fragrances, and the like, look no farther—it's all here.
- *Carousel Clothing Store*
  149 Circuit Avenue
  Oak Bluffs, MA 02557
  (508) 693–9251
- *Martha's Vineyard Resort & Racquet Club*
  Claudette Niles Robins (Inn Keeper)
  P.O. Box 255
Boston, MA 02130
(800) 874–4403

Deluxe bed and breakfast and resort located in Oak Bluffs. The only B&B with its own private recreational facilities.

The Fine Art of Looking Good While Do-Gooding

American Indian College Fund
National Headquarters
1111 Osage Street
Building D, Suite 205W
Denver, CO 80204
(303) 892–8312

The American Indian College Fund is organized to support scholarships and other development needs at tribal colleges (similar to the UNCF).

The Congressional Black Foundation
1004 Pennsylvania Avenue SE
Washington, DC 20003
(202) 675–6730

The foundation's mission is to assist the leaders of today while helping to prepare a new generation of leaders for the future.

Hello Friend
Ennis William Cosby Foundation
P.O. Box 4061
Santa Monica, CA 90411
www.Hellofriend.org

The Hello Friend/Ennis William Cosby Foundation was established to celebrate the life and fulfill the goals and dreams of Ennis William Cosby. His common greeting to friends old and new inspired the name of the foundation.

Jackie Robinson Foundation
3 West 35th Street
New York, NY 10001
(212) 290–8600

The foundation perpetuates the legacy of Jackie Robinson by providing scholarships for minority youths.

Jesse Owens Foundation
401 N. Michigan
Chicago, IL 60611
(312) 527–3311

The foundation seeks to perpetuate the spirit and beliefs of Jesse Owens by supporting educational and social programs that help young people develop their talents, broaden their horizons, and become better citizens. In particular, the foundation helps individuals with the ambition, dedication, and courage to achieve success against significant personal odds.

The Magic Johnson Foundation, Inc.
600 Corporate Pointe, Suite 1080
Culver City, CA 90230
1 (888) MAGIC–05

The foundation awards grants to community-based organizations that create educational, health, and social programs for America's youth.

NAACP
4805 Mt. Hope Drive
Baltimore, MD 21215
(410) 521–4939

The NAACP, the oldest, largest, and strongest civil rights organization in the United States, was founded to ensure the political, educational, social, and economic equality of minority group citizens of the United States.

NAACP Legal Defense and Educational Fund, Inc.
99 Hudson Street, 16th Floor
New York, NY 10013
(212) 219–1900

LDF was founded in 1940 under the leadership of the late Thurgood Marshall, who later became the first Black justice on the United States Supreme Court. (Although initially affiliated with the NAACP, the Legal Defense Fund was always an independent organization. Since 1957, LDF has been completely separate from the NAACP, with its own budget, board of directors, staff, and program.)

National Minority AIDS Council
1931 13th Street NW
Washington, DC 20009
(202) 483—6622

Established in 1987, the organization is committed to developing leadership within communities of color to address the challenge of HIV/AIDS.

The National Urban League
120 Wall Street
New York, NY 10005
(212) 558—5300

This is the premier social services and civil rights organization in America. The Urban League is organized to help African-Americans achieve social and economic equality.

Sickle Cell Association, Inc.
870 N. Military Highway, Suite 316
Fairfax, VA 23502
(757) 466—0332

Association dedicated to providing comprehensive community health education, counseling, and testing for sickle cell disease.

UNCF
8260 Willow Oaks Corporate Drive
Fairfax, VA 22031
(703) 205—3400

The nation's oldest and most successful African-American higher education assistance organization. "A mind is a terrible thing to waste."

Globetrotting for Fun and Excitement

National Alliance of Black School Educators
2816 Georgia Avenue NW
Washington, DC 20001
(202) 483–1549
E-mail: nabse@nabse.org
　　A 5,000-plus member organization founded by Dr. Charles Moody and others. The nation's largest network of African-American educators, it is dedicated to improving the educational accomplishments of African-American youth.

National Association of Black Accountants, Inc.
7249-A Hanover Parkway
Greenbelt, MD 20770
(301) 474–NABA
　　A national professional association whose purpose is to develop, encourage, and serve as a resource for African-American and other minorities' greater participation in the accounting and finance professions.

National Association of Black Journalists
8701A Adelphi Road
Adelphi, MD 20783–1716
(301) 445–7100
　　This is the largest media organization in the world for people of color. With 74 affiliate chapters and 54 student chapters, NABJ is committed to strengthening the ties among African-American journalists.

National Bar Association
1225 11th Street NW
Washington, DC 20001–4217
(202) 842–3900

During the first quarter of the twentieth century, twelve African-American pioneers with a mutual interest in and dedication to justice and the civil rights of all helped structure the struggle of the African-American race in America. The National Bar Association (NBA), formally organized in Des Moines, Iowa, on August 1, 1925, was conceived by George H. Woodson, S. Joe Brown, Gertrude E. Rush, James B. Morris, Charles P. Howard, Sr., Wendell E. Green, C. Francis Stradford, Jesse N. Baker, William H. Haynes, George C. Adams, Charles H. Calloway, and L. Amasa Knox.

National Black MBA Association, Inc.
NBMBAA National Headquarters
180 N. Michigan Avenue, Suite 1400
Chicago, IL 60601
(312) 236–BMBA (2622)

The NBMBAA is a business organization that leads in the creation of economic and intellectual wealth for the Black community.

National Dental Association
3517 16th Street NW
Washington, DC 20010
(202) 588–1697

The National Dental Association (NDA) is the largest and oldest organization of minority oral health professionals in the world. Representing over 7,000 African-American dentists in the United States and abroad, the NDA has become a powerful voice for the health care rights of the underserved. The NDA was formed in 1913 as a forum for practicing African-American dentists who were denied membership in other oral health organizations.

National Medical Association
1012 Tenth Street NW
Washington, DC 20001
(202) 347–1895

The National Medical Association (NMA) is the collective voice of African-American physicians and the leading force for parity and justice in medicine and the elimination of disparities in health.

Membership Is Priceless

Sigma Pi Phi, also known as the Boule, is the oldest African-American professional fraternity in the United States. This organization was founded in 1904, when African-Americans were barred from white clubs. The national organization has a membership of over 3,000 in more than 100 chapters.

The National Association of Guardsmen is a purely social organization. Founded in 1933, the Guardsmen is comprised of eighteen chapters with locations throughout the country. The organization is known particularly for their lavish all-expenses-paid weekends for its members and guests.

BAP SPEAK

Abfab adj. Short for absolutely fabulous

Act out v. phrase To misbehave in public

Activity Vitae n. A BAP's social activity resume or curriculum vitae

A-fie n. The Alpha Phi Alpha Fraternity, Inc. chant that members use to identify one another

African derriere n. The rather shapely African-American butt

Alvin Ailey Dance n. The premier dance troupe founded by Alvin Ailey, now led by Judith Jamison. A dance company that values the neo-African derriere

Artsy-fartsy adj. See granola; crunchy-acting art type

Baby hair n. Shorter hair that frames one's face; sometimes called moonrisers

BAMA n./adj. Individuals known for their backward ways; country; socially inept; tacky

Bankhead Bounce n. A silly dance from the early '90s where your shoulders and body just bounce up and down

BAParent n. The mother or father of a BAP

BAPcard n. A figurative membership in an exclusive group identifiable by choice in clothing and accoutrements, or manner and general demeanor

BAPdom n. The world of BAPs and all its attendant fun

BAPitude adj. The aptitude and attitude of BAPs

Barista n. An individual who prepares beverages at coffee shops

Bébé n. "Baby" in French.

Big sisters n. The name by which members of a sorority must be addressed by the pledges

Birkies n. Short for Birkenstocks

Black & Gold Ball n. Formal dance sponsored by Alpha Phi Alpha Fraternity, Inc.

Bogner n. Designer ski apparel

Bohemian adj. One who does what she feels

Bon vivant n. phrase. A lover of the "good life"

Boomerang BAP n. A BAP who returns to her parents' home after she's been out on her own; she returns just as a boomerang does

Booty n. Behind, butt, tail feather, gluteus maximums

Boy n. Your home slice, your ace, not your boyfriend; ace-boon-coon; a close male friend you can trust

BUPPY n. Black Urban Professional; an individual who has attained success in his/her chosen profession

BWOC n. Big Woman on Campus—what all BAPs are by their mere presence

Chitterlings n. Pig intestines, a holiday favorite which stinks up the house like nobody's business

Compulsive Shopping Disorder n. An affliction of the affluent set, the need to shop 'til you drop, and drop, and drop

Country cousin n. You know you have one—that cousin who reminds you of just how far you have come, and how far you could fall

Creep v. A nice way of saying booty call; creeping occurs on college campuses

Curl n. The most evil hairdo of all time, also known as the Jheri, S, Hawaiian curl, a drippy mess that smelled horrendous

Curlers n. Rollers; used to give hair bounce and body; sometimes worn to maintain a hairstyle

Daimler n. Daimler—the original name for Mercedes-Benz, aka DaimlerChrysler

Dean of pledges n. The sorority sister in charge of the line of women pledging

Debutante n. Young woman in her late teens ready to be presented to society

Dozens n. Game whose champion cracks the best jokes on other participants, rendering them speechless

Fess v. To confess

Fingerwaves n. aka pineapple waves. A sticky mess of waves plastered to the scalp that an atom bomb could not destroy

Fly adj. Hip; très cool

FOB n. Friend of Bill; part of Bill Clinton's inner circle

Funky adj. Very, very cool

Funky-fresh adj. Very, very, very cool

GDI n. Goddamn individual, usually a person who didn't feel the need to pledge to a sorority or fraternity

Ghetto adj. A mode of acting, dressing, or speaking that comes off as abrasive and, well, ghetto

Girl n. A very good friend; short for "girlfriend"

Go kizzy v. phrase. When one's hair looks closer to its natural state than its modern, straightened state; i.e., when it rains outside and your hair rises and naps up

Granola adj. See artsy-fartsy—a crunchy type who loves Birkies and Indian print clothes; a Boho

Greek organizations n. College sororities and fraternities; Alpha Kappa Alpha Sorority, Inc. (AKA); Delta Sigma Theta Sorority, Inc. (DST); Alpha Phi Alpha Fraternity, Inc. (Alphas); Kappa Alpha Psi Fraternity, Inc. (Kappas); Omega Phi Psi Fraternity, Inc. (Omegas)

Greens n. Collards, mustards, a staple of soul food, like spinach; often eaten with hot sauce, cornbread, tomatoes, onions, and vinegar

Groove v. To feel the music; to get in the flow of the music

Ham hock n. The knee of a pig, another soul food staple, mainly used for flavoring and inducing heart attacks

HBCU n. Historically Black Colleges and Universities

Heathen adj. An uncultured person

Hi-hat n. The two cymbals that clap together in a drum set

Hit the blues and greens v. phrase. To ski down the intermediate and beginner slopes

Home training n. Proper upbringing, breeding

Hoopty n. A raggedy car; a beater; an old, beat-up car

Horizontal mambo n. Sex, plain and simple

It n. What you shouldn't touch while with a man unless you're ready to do the deed

Ivy League n. A group of prestigious colleges originally known for being in the same athletic conference; now seen as very special or great schools, aka, "ivies"

Jacked-up adj. Roughly groomed; entirely unkempt

Jams n. Favorite songs

Joe n. A good ole cup of coffee

Jump double dutch v. phrase. A style of jumping rope with two ropes; most BAPs can't do it, but your country cousins can teach you

Kay-A-Sigghhh n. Chant the Kappas say at fraternity and sorority parties to identify themselves

Kente cloth n. Colorful African cloth from Ghana

Kilts n. Short skirts worn during field hockey and lacrosse games

Kinks n. What we refer to our hair as being when it is difficult to manage; a euphemism for naps

---

Koofi n. An African-style hat resembling a Jackie O. pillbox

Locks n. Hairstyle where the hair is twisted into coils and left to grow; a nickname for dreadlocks

Maalox n. Betty's favorite snack, a drug needed for ulcers caused by stress

Meharry n. One of the first African-American medical schools in the country

Mr. Right n. The man, Prince Charming; potential husband; spouse

Mr. Right Now n. The guy you go out with while waiting for Mr. Right; a playa playa or someone to date, but not marriage material

Naps n. Hair that is difficult to comb; kinky hair; unmanageable hair

Neo-BAP n. BAPgirl

New potatoes n. Small-minded people

Now and Later n. Ghetto starbursts

Ooooooh oop n. The chant the DSTs say at fraternity parties to iden-tify themselves

"Operation Getting Over" n. What every kid on vacation with her par-ents tries to institute in order to have more fun than her parents will allow

Parental adj. Of or having to do with parents

"Parler un petit peu de francais" v. phrase. French makes you seem so sophisticated, even if that's all you can say; translated literally, "to speak a little French"

Passion of the hotcomb n. To go *au naturel* with your hair

P.C. adj. phrase. Politically correct

Petit bourgeoisie adj. French term for the middle class

Pledge v. The process of joining a sorority or fraternity, aka "on line"; the line must act as one for the length of the pledge process

Prima donna adj. A narcissistic diva

Raggedy adj. Old and beat-up

Relax hair v. To straighten one's hair; for the last time, Black people do not get perms, we get relaxers

Rite of Passage n. A ceremony for African-American children that marks their transition into adulthood

Ruff-Ruff n. A chant the Omega Psi Phi Fraternity members say at fraternity and sorority parties to identify themselves

Sanka n. Decaf coffee

Sassy adj. A word often associated with Black women to indicate spunk and verve, often misused and overused when we tell the truth

Shake one's tail feather v. To dance

Shake the groove thing v. phrase. To dance

shakus groovethangus n. A dance affliction that overcomes students at high noon on college campuses

Shellac baby hair v. phrase. Slapping down the baby hair on your face with grease so you look like a moron

Show out v. To misbehave in public

Skeeee-wee n. The AKA chant, somewhat piercing to the ear

Smush v. To cuddle, to spoon

Soror n. A sorority sister

Spoon v. Make your body fit into the shape of your partner's while cuddling. Stack yourselves like spoons

Stacy Adams n. A tacky shoe worn by old men with few sartorial sensibilities; a ghetto favorite

"Su casa es mi casa." Spanish phrase meaning "Your house is my house" (aka the BAParent home to the BAP)

Sweet potatoes n. aka, yams, boiled with sugar; tastes so good it makes you want to slap your grandma; a metaphor for a BAP's Black world

Tail feather n. Behind; butt; booty

Throw down v. To be a virtuoso in the kitchen

Tootsie Roll n. A ghetto dance

Twists n. Pre-dreads, natural hair twisted into little coils

Upsweep hairdo n. A ghetto hairstyle where the hair is shaped around a foam bubble and gel is applied so that the hair does not move

Vs adj. An abbreviation for the rating of diamonds—very slight inclusions

Walk in line v. phrase. While pledging, the line must act as one; pledges must do everything together in unison, even walking down the street

Weave n. When hair is sewn onto your real hair that is braided to your scalp to create a new look or hairstyle; or to give your hair a rest

Wedgwood n. One of the oldest tableware makers in the world, very exclusive and expensive

Work one's nerve v. phrase. To irritate someone

Zagat n. Premier restaurant guide available in major cities

About the Authors

Kalyn Johnson is an associate at a large law firm in New York. **Tracey Lewis** is a writer. **Karla Lightfoot** is an advertising sales executive in New York. **Ginger Wilson,** a Chicago attorney, is the executive director of a legal staffing firm.

Jane Archer is an illustrator who works in book publishing in New York City. To see more of her work, visit her on the Web at janearcher illustration.com